Praise For *Prison Baby*

"*Prison Baby* hits all the emotions of the who, what, where, when and why of adoption right on the head of the nail! Some real deep life stuff is in these pages. It stirs the soul. . . . If you want to know the truth about finding who you really are, this is the story! Adopted or not."

—Darryl "DMC" McDaniels,
adoptee and founder of the hip-hop group Run-DMC

"Deborah Jiang Stein has beaten the cycle of intergenerational incarceration, despite the odds against her—multiracial, born in a federal prison to a heroin-addicted mother. Her story offers hope to the possibility of personal transformation for anyone. No punches pulled. Deborah is evidence of the magnificent resilience of the human spirit."

—Sister Helen Prejean,
author of *Dead Man Walking* and Pulitzer Prize nominee

"*Prison Baby*, one woman's profound quest for family and identity, is also a soul-stirring call to arms on behalf of incarcerated women and their children. It's a story of lost-and-found, conflict-and-peace, and proof that—with love, forgiveness, and support—people really do change their lives."

—Tayari Jones,
author of *Silver Sparrow*

"A profoundly moving search for identity, *Prison Baby* is as inspiring as it is haunting. Deborah Jiang Stein's bold and intrepid honesty will speak to anyone who has struggled with grief, forgiveness, and finding his or her place in the world."

—Katrina Kittle,
author of *The Blessings of the Animals*

"At a time when more and more women are being incarcerated worldwide, Deborah Jiang Stein's story of the secrets and ignominy surrounding her prison birth gives readers a brave account of the backlash children and society encounter when families are torn apart by addiction, prison, and shame. More than anything, Deborah's book is a call for an open-eyed examination of our broken criminal justice system and a heartfelt plea for more compassionate responses to poverty and mental illness."

—Naseem Rakha,
author of *The Crying Tree*

"*Prison Baby* is an emotionally charged, transformative story about one woman's search for her true origins. Candid and searing, Deborah Jiang Stein's memoir is a remarkable story about identity, lost and found, and about the author's journey to reclaim—and celebrate—that most primal of relationships, the one between mother and child. I dare you to read this book without crying."

—Mira Bartok,
author of *The Memory Palace*

"Deborah Jiang Stein's startling journey is impossible to forget. . . . The hidden truth of her birth spurs her into the frightening territory of drugs, crime, and addiction, a crucible from which she miraculously emerges with earned wisdom, insight, and the sheltering love of two families. The ways this woman discovers herself, via the revelation of her birth mother and her reconciliation with her adoptive mother, show us how dramatically different worlds intersect, and why those intersections are so important to who we are. The bonds of mothers and daughters separated by race, class, and even by prison prove too powerful for those formidable barriers and divisions. A powerful story."

—Piper Kerman,
author of *Orange Is the New Black*

PRISON BABY

For Sandy,
Thank you!
Deborah

PRISON BABY

A Memoir

DEBORAH JIANG STEIN

Beacon Press
Boston

BEACON PRESS
Boston, Massachusetts
www.beacon.org

Beacon Press books
are published under the auspices of
the Unitarian Universalist Association of Congregations.

Some names and identifying characteristics of people mentioned
in this work have been changed to protect their identities.

Author's note: The stories in this book are my personal interpretations of thoughts,
feelings, opinions, statements, attitudes, and events as I perceive them, both in the
past and present. All dialogue is written as I recall it. Personal postcards, letters,
and government correspondence are from existing documents.

17 16 15   8 7 6 5 4 3 2

This book is printed on acid-free paper that meets the uncoated
paper ANSI/NISO specifications for permanence as revised in 1992.

Text design and composition by Kim Arney

An earlier version of this book was published as *Even Tough Girls Wear Tutus*
(privately published, 2011).

Library of Congress Cataloging-in-Publication Data
Stein, Deborah.
[Even tough girls wear tutus]
Prison baby : a memoir / Deborah Jiang Stein.
pages   cm
Originally published in 2012 by Cell 7 Media as: Even tough girls wear tutus.
ISBN 978-0-8070-9810-3 (pbk. : alk. paper)
1. Stein, Deborah. 2. Children of women prisoners—United States—Biography.
3. Adopted children—United States—Biography. 4. Racially mixed children—United
States—Biography. 5. Female juvenile delinquents—United States—Biography.
6. Drug addicts—Rehabilitation—United States—Biography. I. Title.
HV9468.S748A3 2014
362.82'95092—dc23
[B]
2013039396

CONTENTS

CHAPTER ONE

THE LETTER

SWEAT GLUES MY PALM TO THE brass knob of my parents' bedroom door.

It's an off-limits, by-invitation-only room, sacred, like a boudoir. We kids don't dare go in on our own. Until today.

It's my first breaking and entering. But what else does a twelve-year-old girl do when she's grounded but sneak around the house?

I listen for a second at the door of their room to make sure no one's in there and then twist the knob. A ray of Seattle's noon sun slants through the glass of the patio door on the far side of the room. I'm glad for that door. Good thing my dad just fixed the sliding device, though. Short on patience, he isn't much of a handyman. Things break in his hands more often than they are repaired. If my parents come in, I can slip my slim five-foot frame out the sliding door and escape.

I creep across the room, around the footboard of their bed, and face my mother's nightstand where a bird book, two novels, and three volumes of poetry pile high against her alarm clock. Her quick-fire brain keeps her engaged in no less than three or four books and magazines at the same time, each one bookmarked midway—*Audubon News*, the Sierra Club magazine, the *New Yorker*, the ACLU newsletter, books about the history of ancient Rome and Greece, poetry.

A mechanical pencil alongside pages of my father's typed manuscript, with scribbled notes in the margins, cover his nightstand. He keeps his dresser top bare except for a tray of pipe and

1

cigar paraphernalia—always a Zippo lighter, pipe cleaners, a box of wooden matches, a pipe damper, and an Italian leather box with gold fleur-de-lis engraved on the outside. Inside, his Italian cufflinks crafted in gold, silver, and leather jumble together.

I tiptoe to my mother's dresser where her clip-on earrings and a strand of pearls scatter across the top. If it weren't for her tray of Chanel bottles and collection of perfume atomizers, I'd have to pinch my nostrils to block the reek of my father's tobacco.

I slide open my mother's top dresser drawer.

"Shhhh," I whisper and grab Kittsy, our Siamese, to quiet the rattle of her purr. Then I set her down and she weaves in and out between my feet, her tail in a fast flicker around my ankles. But the sweep of her purr and her tail across my skin comfort me. She calms my nighttime monster dreams when she nuzzles on my pillow, her belly curved around my head, her almond-shaped eyes more like mine than anyone else's in my family.

The scent of Mother's French soap collection wafts out of her dresser drawer. Each bar, the size of a silver dollar wrapped in parchment paper, perfumes her drawers. Neat stacks of folded underwear and silk slips bunch in a pile at the back of her top drawer.

I glance through the sliding-glass door—nobody's in sight on the other side. Mother's in her garden where she snips dead tulip heads and prunes her rose bed. My father's secluded in his study out back, a room connected to our detached garage. He's always hunched over a manuscript about John Donne or Milton, deep in thought and taking long puffs on either a Cuban cigar or one of his pipes. Jonathan hotdogs on his bike somewhere in the neighborhood with his friends. He's older than me by eighteen months and never in trouble. He leaves the back talk and smarty-pants to his little sister.

Nothing here. I nudge the top drawer closed, but a corner of white catches my eye. A crisp piece of paper peeks out from under the plastic drawer liner, printed with miniature roses.

I peel up a corner of the liner.

Lodged under silky slips, under all the softness and the scent of perfume, stashed like a rumpled stowaway in a first-class cabin, I unveil a copy of a typed letter, just a paragraph long.

My neck throbs—boom da boom—my pulse in a loud pump of anticipation all the way into my shoulder muscles. High and tight as usual, my clenched shoulder blades draw in my neck so much it aches.

Must be important if it's hidden. I already know I'm adopted, so the letter can't be about that. Maybe it's about my race, or races. No one's explained to me why I'm caramel-colored in a white family.

My mother writes to the family attorney:

Can you please alter Deborah's birth certificate from the Federal Women's Prison in Alderson, West Virginia, to Seattle. Nothing good will come from her knowing she lived in the prison before foster care, or that her birth mother was a heroin addict. After all, she was born in our hearts here in Seattle, and if she finds all this out she'll ask questions about the prison and her foster homes before we adopted her.

Impossible. Read it again. Everything blurs.

Foster care? I'd no idea about my life before my adoption or even how old I was at the time or where I lived before then.

I read the letter over and over, these new truths forever imprinted into my memory.

I step back a few paces from the dresser and sink into the folded comforter at the end of my parents' bed.

Prison?

Born in prison? No one's born in a prison.

The worst place, the worst of the worst: prison. And the worst people, from everything I've heard in cartoons and seen in magazines and heard from talk.

I tuck the paper back under the liner and float from the dresser into my parents' bathroom and stare at myself in the mirror over their sink, my body in overload. Time and space distort inside me. I don't know where I am. My feet seem to lift, my body and brain separated by some wedge, and I'm disconnected from my house, from my neighborhood, from Earth, from humanity.

It can't be true. If it is, what's wrong with me? When people find out, then what? Who loves anyone from prison?

My skin itches as if tiny ants crawl along the bones in my forearms, and I scratch so hard red streaks rise on my skin. I splash water onto my burning face but give up after a while. I can't wash away what I know isn't there, but I feel dirty, as if grime coats my cheeks, hot to my hands. Still, I can't stop splashing my face to rinse the grit from my eyes. My mouth has a sour taste.

Then something sinks in. My "real" mother's an addict and a criminal. My "real" home is a prison.

The trauma of learning about my birth sends me into a deep dive, an emotional lockdown behind a wall that imprisons me for almost twenty years. The letter forces me into an impossible choice between two mothers, two worlds far apart. One mother behind bars, a criminal, a drug addict, tugs at me, her face and voice buried deep in my subconscious. The other, the mother I face every day, the one who keeps fresh bouquets of flowers on our teak credenza, I don't connect with this mother.

I'm not hers. Not theirs.

It's the first and last time I read the letter, and I never see it again. I don't need to, for every word is etched in my brain, and it's given me all the proof I need. I'm not the daughter of parents who toss Yiddish quips back and forth, of the mother who spends her Saturday afternoons throwing clay with a pottery teacher, then comes home with darling miniature ceramic vases, the mother who writes poetry with a Mont Blanc fountain pen and uses the same to correct her students' papers. I'm not the daughter of the mother who cans cherries and whips the best whipped cream ever, the mother who says "I love you, Pet" so many times I want to smack her, the mother who waits for me after my ballet class every Saturday.

Don't think about it. It's not true, none of it happened. Not even the letter.

Some things we need to unthink and erase, just to endure living.

That night at dinner, everything moves in slow motion as if on a conveyor belt. The voices of my family echo far away, as if from a faint cave. I forget I've ever read the letter, forget everything in it. Gone. Zip. Out of my mind, and it doesn't show up again until a flash about a month later. Maybe not a month, maybe eight. I forget this too. These new facts about my prison birth never stay in my brain or anywhere inside me long enough to grasp. But something this big can't hide for long. Buried secrets live forever, glued to our insides like sticky rice.

I convince myself: "Don't think of it. Then it's not true."

Thus begins more than a decade of emotional lockdown, a feeling I'd experienced before but never understood what it was.

The anguish seeps out of me like poison trapped in a balloon-sized blister.

My brain battles as I force it to divorce from reality, the one way to metabolize what I've just learned: *I was born in prison.*

CHAPTER TWO

LUCKY

ONE SUMMER WHEN I'M AROUND EIGHT, before I have found the letter, we drive across the country from Seattle to Lake Winnipesaukee, New Hampshire, to vacation with my aunts, uncles, and cousins on my father's side. We often vacation near a lake or the ocean, on the Oregon coast, near our home in Seattle, or as far off as the East Coast.

For as long as I can remember, the power and passion of the ocean captivated me. That first whiff of salted air carved itself into my uncluttered memory, and the sounds of the sea soothed me more than anything. The ocean gives a good reason to feel small in life's landscape, small and yet not out of place the way I feel everywhere else. I can't find the right track to follow for how to live, how to act. Our beach visits offer a refuge, a mysterious peace in the solitude. Water is a pocket of gracious healing. Life is all there, roaring and real, a place for perfect safety.

MY FATHER GREW up in Brockton, Massachusetts, and his two sisters remain on the East Coast, one in New Hampshire, the other in New York. We spend a few weeks together every year at the lake, each family in their own modern log cabin but sharing a common clothesline, picnic table, and stone-rimmed fire circle.

My two uncles, Peter and Marty, hold me in long bear hugs whenever I try to run past them on the way to the beach. Their knock-knock jokes, pranks, and bubbles of love bring me out of my shell. Silly is the furthest thing from my ponderous father, the bearded stoic and scholar who might give a quick swing of his hand upside my head if something I say irritates him or if the energy of my mischief calls forth his reprimands.

Not always. Sometimes. He's unpredictable in his outbursts, and once is enough to live on edge and wonder: Will this call out his wrath?

I thrive around my uncles' playfulness, the same way I thrive around my mother's side of the family in Minneapolis. It's easier to let my guard down with both extended families. They bring me out of my isolation, and it's simple: I just want hugs and to play without a need to perform or pressure for "proper" behavior.

One afternoon my cousin Dorrie bursts through our cabin screen door and races up to me. She's like an older sister to me and born on the same day as my older brother.

"You're lucky!" she exclaims. The door slams behind her because she's run in so fast with her news. "My mother told me you were chosen, said you're lucky because they had to take me just because I was born to them."

I stare at her. *What's lucky about me?*

"You got picked," she says, and spreads her arms wide. "You're adopted." Then she adds, "Lucky!"

This is the first time I've heard the word *adopted*. I don't have a clue what she's talking about or how the word connects to me. All I understand is I think adoption means some kids come from a first set of parents but live with a second set. I'd never thought about why. No one ever told me about my adoption, although I've already sensed something different about me. But I don't know what and haven't figured out why no one looks like me.

I don't feel lucky. I'm sick in my stomach, tight inside, like a rubber-band ball the size of a bowling ball. Just then the screen door of the cabin squeaks and slams again, and my cousin Doug walks in with his wide smile. He always impersonates the "What, me worry?" character from *Mad* magazine, and I giggle every time. Not this time. I stare off past him and walk outside towards the beach. I don't remember much after this. I never said anything to anyone. My usual lockdown took over, an instinct and habit I acquired long before the shock of the letter hit me. Any kind of trauma sent me into this state, but it's impossible to lock up just one experience. The fence I'm building around me is turning into a concrete wall with barbed wire at the top.

I waited until we arrived home from New Hampshire to pull out more details from my mother about my adoption. Shortly after we return, I track her down in our garden on a late Saturday afternoon. She's sleeveless and wrist deep in planting tulips, geraniums, and pansies, and yanking weeds, her usual for the weekend. The garden is the one "room" I like to share with my mother. I never let on how I admire her strength, the way she pounds stakes to prop up her plants or untangles a garden hose as it whips around the yard when she sets the sprinkler near her shrubs.

A late afternoon mist has moved in as the Seattle sun prepares to settle.

"Am I adopted?" I ask.

"Yes, you're adopted." Her answer drops with a thump and sticks like flour to wet glass. In and out, her jaw muscles clench.

She digs lines of holes for tulip bulbs and doesn't return my gaze. "And we love you."

Inside I'm a swirl: *Tell me everything! Who is she? My mother, my other mother, why didn't she want me? Where is she?*

Silence weighs heavy in the air. I need her to say more, but I don't know how to ask. I keep it all in. I hold my breath and gnaw the inside of my cheek, too afraid, too frozen inside to dare.

It's true. I have two mothers. Another mother, somewhere else.

The final question pounds at my insides: Didn't she want me?

Most adopted kids wonder about the same question. Kids simplify, and for many adopted children it goes like this, a belief in our rawest core: if we're good, they want us, and if we're bad, they give us away.

The deeper my mother digs in the dirt, the more hatred is dredged up in me. Mother-blame sets in. I hate her for her brief answer, hate her for adopting me, and hate myself for being adopted. Nothing bothers me about the identity of my birth father. Not yet. It's primal, the complex bond between a mother and daughter. *Why didn't my prison mother keep me? Didn't she want me? If I love Mother, am I betraying my other mother? But isn't she the one who didn't want me?* I try not to think about this.

The more muddled and saddened I feel about losing my prison mom, the more I hate Mother. I cringe every time she says those words—"we love you"—and every hug adds to the hate.

MY BROTHER, JONATHAN, was adopted at birth and is almost two years older than I am and Caucasian. For much of my childhood, I didn't know he was adopted, perhaps because he didn't seem to suffer in the same ways I did. For some reason I just accepted him as my brother, maybe because I didn't have another brother. He was it. I loved him as my protector and hated him for it at the same time. I hated his whiteness and felt jealous of it. I hated his boy-ness, his handsome-ness, his charisma and social ease. I hated his favored standing in the eyes of my parents. And I loved him.

Light-olive-colored skin gave him the look of an Italian boy, with all the verbal and charismatic traits of a first-born. While my grades were sometimes higher than my brother's, Jonathan was an affable young man—the polar opposite of his moody, timid sister. I'm the one who stretched the rules. Jonathan was bar mitzvahed and was a track star in school. He wore a confident attitude and fitted pants and t-shirts that showed off his muscles. We got along well, though our musical tastes clashed. He played the Beach Boys and surfer music of the 1960s. I cranked up Aretha, James Brown, the Temptations, Marvin Gaye, and Nina Simone.

My parents sent Jonathan to comfort me whenever I couldn't stop one of my crying jags. Sometimes I'd sob and sob and sob until my throat muscles felt like they'd snap. He'd sit by my side and pat my back, and I'd calm down, simple as that. I remember him saying, "It's all right," even though "it" wasn't all right, and I didn't know what "it" was. His tenderness helped. I knew he loved me.

Every week after Sunday school, my mother and brother and I stopped at the Twenty-Third Street Bakery in the inner-city Central District, the only Black neighborhood in Seattle. While my mother ran in to pick up snacks for us, we waited outside in her faded-green Plymouth.

One Sunday Jonathan grabbed my shoulder and shoved me under the front seat of the car. I was still small enough to fit under it. He whispered in a panic: "I'll lock the doors! They might take you!"

By "they," I knew he meant someone whose skin color matched mine more than his. My t-shirt tore over my brown-skinned back from where the coiled car-seat springs stuck out.

Whenever someone walked by the car, he repeated his order, as if a Black family would take me away. Like me, he wasn't sure in which world I belonged, but I knew he loved me with his big-brother protectiveness.

When Mother got into the car with a bag of doughnuts, Jonathan grabbed for the sugar and glazed ones, but I wanted to run away in our yard to climb trees, seclusions high in the sky.

MY FIRST MEMORY in my adoptive family is a recurring dream. The dream goes like this: From high above, I'm looking down on myself right before sleep descends in the bedroom I share with Jonathan. The room is dark, other than the nightlight by the roofless wooden dollhouse by my bed. Just when my spirit is about to leave my body and float around the world, a vision startles me. Five or so unrecognizable faces of women surround me in a half-circle. We are in a room full of movement, a busier environment than the sedate atmosphere of my childhood home. In this mirage, the onlookers' faces, sometimes visible and other times obscured behind vertical lines, peer down at me as I rest on my bed. Narrow wooden rods hide their bodies below the shoulder. I wake soon after I fall asleep, the dream so brief.

The same women stand around me every night. I'm not distressed; I just feel crowded, my personal space invaded. I crave solitude. I wake up weepy, not fearful about the dream but, rather, sad about its recurrence, the repetition of images I can't understand. I sniffle in the night so no one will hear.

Jonathan, asleep in his bed on the other side of the room, has no idea what's going on. He's a deep sleeper and never hears me stir or cry in the night.

MY RECURRING DREAM haunted me for years. I call it my crib dream, the vertical lines maybe crib rods from my past. I couldn't shake the dream and even grew to expect it every night. After a while, the dream women at the edge of my bed stood like a wall between the world and me. They never left, yet I can't identify who they were. When my brother and I moved upstairs into our converted attic bedrooms when I was around age seven or so, though, I never dreamed the vision again.

After I unearthed the news about my roots, I began to wonder if my dream vision had started in prison with my birth mother and other inmates, the vertical lines representing iron window guards and not crib rods. Or was the image a memory from one of my foster homes?

I have no idea if Mother heard me cry—whether it was from my bedwetting, even as a grade-school girl, or from my angst about waking up in the morning with my thumb in my mouth—but I knew she cared for me in the night. I longed to stop wetting my bed and sucking my thumb, tried and tried and just couldn't. Not until my teens.

Many times after I'd woken up crying, I'd sit up, lean over the edge of my bed, grip my pillow so I wouldn't fall out, and grope around in the dark for the single graham cracker my mother would hide each night in one of the rooms of the dollhouse next to my bed. The tooth fairy also visited the same dollhouse rooms the nights after I lost a tooth.

I'd discover my treasure and then sit up in bed and nibble it, one hand under my chin to catch the crumbs. The crackers appeared night after night, yet my mother and I never discussed this secret ritual. I locked my tenderness inside.

Memory can play tricks on us. Or maybe we trick memory to serve a deeper purpose. Maybe I kept the dream alive so I could keep the sensation of my prison mother surrounding me.

The longer I kept her with me, the more I pushed away Mother, the one I should have loved, the one I wasn't sure I wanted to love. The longer I kept myself outside my family, the more I lived with the memory sensations of my first home in prison. I'd begun to glamorize my birth mother, to romanticize our relationship, romanticize the prison and whatever sent her there.

The longing stayed with me, but I didn't know for what. I couldn't control any of it.

CHAPTER THREE

RIVER OF QUIET

MY ELEMENTARY SCHOOL TEACHERS SEND ME to the principal's office at least three times a week. One day I pull the fire alarm, another day I hide above the dropped-ceiling tiles and jump on top of my teacher. Bits of sheetrock rain down on her as I thump onto her desk. On another day I sit on a boy's lap in the first row, and on a different day I wave the blue-gold flame of my stolen Zippo lighter, my favorite score from my parents' bedroom, over toilet paper rolls and crumpled wads of paper towels in the girls' bathroom trash can. No false fire drill this time.

All the trouble I stir makes me forget about the prison, forget the fact of my birthplace. It's gone from my consciousness, but deep inside, a river of quiet anguish runs through me.

My gut's in a constant tangle, and Mother drags me, trip after trip, to the doctor's office for my stomachaches.

"Nothing wrong," the doctor says on a visit.

She and my mother discuss bland foods.

Nothing wrong? This isn't a food problem. *What about the big prison secret?*

It's one of the random days I remember I was born in prison.

They're all crazy. Everything's wrong.

All the wrong out there, I store deep inside a cave, and stay mute for days at a time, day after day after day. No one can get to my deepest feelings.

My mother doesn't miss a beat in her mission to groom me into refinement. Piano and French lessons, Hebrew in Sunday school, swim-team workouts where I train in the butterfly and breast stroke, and a two-week modeling class. It's like forced servitude inside a world of arts and civility, tea and classical music, hours on hours of traipsing around the Seattle Art Museum, when my instinct wants to run free and play and prank. Prancy by nature. At the same time I find peace in art and music. Our family ritual of tea at night is way too civil.

But my ballet on the weekend . . . Every Saturday afternoon from the time I'm in third grade, my mother walks me to the last house on our dead-end street where I sashay across the oak floor in the basement of our neighbor's homemade dance studio and do grand plié at the ballet bar.

I love the freedom and silence of dance. The classical music, the meditation, and the athleticism all ease a struggle I later learn relates to sensory-integration issues often triggered in drug-exposed children. The shiny, varnished oak floor, the bright reflection of the sun on the mirrored walls, everything makes life better for the hour I'm cocooned in the studio filled with sweat and fluorescent lights. Most of all, I love my pink tutu and love grinding the leather of my ballet slippers into the dusty box of resin.

Dance is my relief from feeling abnormal, an escape from the angst. No one's told me what race I am, yet I see I'm weird because nobody else in my world is brown with white parents. I already know I'm adopted, but what else? And why am I a different color than my parents? I need answers.

MY PARENTS TAKE my brother and me to the theater, ballet, modern-dance performances, poetry readings, museums, and everything kooky and experimental in the arts. The magic of dance and mime touch my soul more than anything, then or now. It started when I was around eight. I'd dream of theater and movement, mime and dance, from the moment I sat in a darkened theater with my parents and Marcel Marceau tiptoed on stage in his white ballet shoes and mimed inside an invisible box.

But I'm sure I don't belong in the world of dance or theater. Apart from my love of dance, I'm a tomboy, and besides, the ballerinas on stage and the dolls in stores only have blonde hair. Not light caramel-brown skin or wavy black hair like mine, so thick it volumizes into troll-doll hair whenever the humidity spikes. It's the 1960s, long before Alvin Ailey and Judith Jamison have shown the world ballet isn't just for white people.

Besides, how can I flit around in the dance studio like a fairy or dream of grand jetés across the big stage with red velvet curtains if my dance teacher—if anyone—ever finds out my secret? The more I suppress it, the more profoundly I believe I'm a bad girl. I think being prison-born means I need to walk tough in the world.

I ALSO CRAVE adventure.

Spring leaps into the first day of summer, liberating me from sixth grade. It's before I find the letter.

Away from the confines of my house and family, I'm emancipated and brave, not the timid, compliant, and sometimes mute little girl my family thinks I am. Whenever I'm out on some adventure in the neighborhood, my mother's words that boil my blood—"you're one of us"—disappear. It's magic. She's gone. My family's gone. My school and the kids with their jeers of "ching-chong" and taunts of pulled eyes, all gone.

One day I head to a neighbor's house across the street where they've just finished building a ten-foot-high retaining wall. Cement still damp, it calls to me.

I tread across the dewy lawn and plant both feet firmly on the concrete where the grass meets the top of the wall. The back of my tennis shoes hang into the grass.

Heights jumble my guts, but I'd do anything—even fly to the moon and back if I could—to dance on the hairline between fear and excitement. I leap. I fly. I drink in every blast of adrenaline as if my very life depends on it.

Inch forward, I tell myself. Then I lift a foot, ready to jut my toes over the wall's edge. My rubber soles slip, still slick from the moist grass, and the fear of falling fires panic in me. My stomach pulls tight. The world around me vaporizes and my head fills with the fervor for risk and fun: danger-fun. My whole universe right up to the edge of this second disappears. The rush of adrenaline drowns out everything else—my past, my pain, even the lock-down. Rather than quiver in terror, I'm at peace in the face of fear and excitement.

I slide on the wall up to the arches of my feet. Adrenaline rips through me and crackles my world open, my senses on fire. I inhale the whole neighborhood—chlorine from my best friend Wendy's pool next door, dog poop in someone's backyard, fumes from the Ferrari revving at the end of the block. The crack of a baseball across the yard means Jonathan won't check on his little sister. It all mingles in my lungs and floods me as I teeter on top of the wall.

No one's around as I teeter on the wall. Just how I like it. I'm not here to impress anyone. I'd rather daredevil alone.

Petrified to even peek over the wall ledge, I pace back and forth on top across its six-foot length. Then I lean to gaze past the brink onto the hard-packed dirt below. The soles of my tennis shoes, now dry and squeaky, catch on the concrete. I stumble. Back away. My heart pumps and swells into a bowling ball in my chest. Terror and excitement clash inside me.

Better sit, I tell myself, and plop on top of the wall and dangle my feet. I press my palms into the concrete nubs, bend at my waist to peer down, and dig my nail-bitten fingertips into the edge, not much to grip onto. So I push the heels of my shoes into a crevice in the wall to stabilize. Then I lean over farther to gauge where the concrete meets earth.

Almost sick to my stomach from the jumble of fear and anticipation, I pop up to my feet. My mother's voice rings in my head: Be more careful, dear.

"Careful" is not part of me unless I'm around my family, my teachers, or my mother, and only then does caution seep into me like an oozy infection.

A few kids, mostly boys, gather below me. They dig in the dirt with sticks and fling pebbles against the wall. Behind them a swing-set sits empty. Lobe-leafed ivy grips a fence. A songbird perches on top and flaps its wings in a dance to the da-da-da-dat da-da-da-dat of a jackhammer from a few houses away. Maybe there's another wall under construction for me to climb. Pretty soon some boys from next door run over to join the kids at the bottom of the wall and they all toss their heads back to look up.

I squat down a bit as if to high dive off the end of a diving board, then swing my arms forward and fly, feet first. I whoop with glee and the kids hoot and howl. One of the boys jumps up and down and shouts: Do it again!

Yes, do it again, I tell myself in the split second after I hit the dirt. I'm high from the flight and relieved to land, yet at the same time hate how my feet must ever touch ground again. Why can't I soar into eternity? Maybe I was born in the wrong body—meant to fly, not walk.

My courage balloons with the claps and cheers, the kids egging me on.

"Anyone wanna try with me?" I ask my audience. No takers.

"You go again!" a boy shouts. He pumps his fist in the air.

I race up the grassy slope to the corner where the wall meets the house. This time, with no pause, as soon as I reach the top and without one look down, arms out in a perfect second position—a T—head high, in my longest stride, I step straight into space. Three quick steps of walking on air! Then I plummet down.

CHAPTER FOUR

ON THE EDGE

I LAND ON MY FEET AS ALWAYS. When each succeeding jump grows duller, the one thrill left catches my eye on my last flight through air: a flurry of snapdragons and purple and yellow pansies in the garden. They beam their happy-smile faces at me. Beauty blurs with speed but nothing equals my first thrill, alive on the edge.

I'll do anything to soar in the air and feed this adrenaline rush, where something drives me to take risks, to jump from heights, from a tree, a wall, the small cliff down the street from our house, from on top of the swing set in our backyard, a rooftop, the moon. I need the high, the fire in me between fear and fun. It also helps calm the bounce in my brain.

It happens anywhere, most often at school or at home. Ideas ripple behind my eyes as if a tsetse fly had burrowed there and infested my senses. Sometimes thoughts tumble through my brain and I can't connect them in order. Then, it's free-for-all fun inside my head where my wires spark wild and crossed. It can happen when people talk, when I write, or when I read. It can happen when I speak. My imagination chases a phrase somewhere and I might not come back in time to catch the next sentence. The flow, the meaning, sails away. Then I'm in sensory overload and sentences swim. My thinking turns into a cut-and-paste collage and once I put the pieces together, a slow-motion static buzzes in a hive inside where I need to decode and unscramble key words, phrases, sentences. Everything mashes together while I patch the full meaning into something that makes sense. How can just twenty-six letters in the alphabet whirl up such pandemonium?

None of this is good for a daughter with a scholar for a father who lectures us kids, not yet double-digit ages, in sentences a paragraph long and addresses us as if we're graduate students in his advanced seminar on *Paradise Lost*, the epic poem to which he devotes his entire career as a literary critic. As an undergrad at Yale, my father's advisor suggested he not write about Milton for his thesis because, as my father tells the story, "How could a Jew understand Milton?" Yale and Harvard once had a quota of ten percent Jews. As it turns out, my father ended up an expert on Milton and was asked later to teach in their summer schools.

I DON'T ALWAYS let on when I need help but my teachers reexplain homework assignments until I understand. It just takes their patience, with a hand on my shoulder and one extra try. Or two tries. Or five. Sometimes I just pretend I understand.

Whenever a teacher stands next to my desk and drapes her arm across my back, I lean an inch closer to her side and breathe easier as my lungs fill with a puff of billowy clouds. My insides shift and the taut rubber-band ball in me bounces out, at least for the moment.

I love a teacher's arm around me while she tells me what to do. I'm starved for physical affection since I won't let my mother close to me. I long more for my birth mother's arm on my back. Forever.

I want my teachers to take care of me, and I make a silent vow to them: *I'll always behave how you want and promise to follow rules. I'll be good.*

Even more than attention from my teachers, though, I love hanging around Eloise, my mother's best friend, and the mother of my best friend, Wendy. Weekends I dash down our driveway and across the street to their house. They're my favorite family and I want to spend all my time there. Not because of their swimming pool and horses, but to escape from my house. Wendy's father, affectionate and soft-spoken, is a Superior Court judge and later a state legislator, and he never minds if any of us kids run or yell in their house. Eloise never makes demands on me to speak or do anything. I don't want her as my mother, but sometimes I wish she were because I just want to be near her warmth.

I often grow enamored of other women, other mothers, even my teachers, and I wish to belong to them, to any motherly woman whose tender encouragement frees me inside.

Things feel simpler with Eloise. She doesn't try to engage me in conversation, and I follow her around her house, from the kitchen to the living room, and she never seems to mind. She includes me in her baking and snack preparations, and hosts elaborate Easter egg hunts for the neighborhood kids. Though we're the only Jewish family in the neighborhood, Mother sends us over to their yard to dive into the bushes and look for colored eggs with the other kids.

ELOISE THREW BIRTHDAY parties for Wendy and her older sister, Gini, and their brother, Frankie, with cupcakes and wrapping paper strewn on the floor and friends over, too. They were nothing like the more formal birthday dinners with my family, where we celebrated with just the four of us. My heart always ached on my birthday. I'd sit on the fireplace hearth and hold back tears, watch my mother set the dinner table for my birthday dinner, and yearn for a fun birthday. But I couldn't stop my sadness. At the same time, I felt sorry for Mother because she wanted me cheery on my birthday.

I GROW UP at my father's side watching Friday night fights on television. His Brockton hometown is famous for boxers, Rocky Marciano and Marvin Hagler. I plop my sixty-pound skinny self in a chair next to him, his six-foot-four frame sprawled on the couch. My mother hates the violence of boxing, and Jonathan prefers his model cars or painting watercolors in the solitude of our bathroom, his makeshift art studio.

Even though my father's ready rage—often for no apparent reason related to me—and the thunder of his voice makes me cower, I look forward to the boxing matches on TV with him, look forward to a time to sit together without having to talk. I love the smack of the boxers' shoes in their dance against the canvas. The bell, the referee's modulated announcements, the ringside shouts from the crowd, the boxers' deep huffs for air, sweat raining down their faces, the Vaseline dabbed on open wounds between rounds, and the pound of glove smacks. Every sound pierces through the TV screen and it all makes me want to box, to jump in the ring and fight, to burst out in an explosion.

After the ref's opening instruction—"Now touch gloves, then go to your corners, and come out fighting"—my father's running commentary on the rounds is the one time the boom of his voice doesn't alarm me.

"Good right!" my father shouts and pitches forward, his elbow propped on his knees.

"Keep 'em up!" he coaches a weary boxer to raise his gloves and protect his face. "That's it! Wear him out. Just keep 'em up!"

As a young man, my father boxed in amateur bouts, his lanky and lean less-than-two-hundred-pound body perfect for the sport. He believed in the balance of exercise to complement the hours he spent in mental discipline. He taught me the old adage: all work and no play and exercise make us dull. Even though my father devoted hours to the study of seventeenth-century literature and was a dedicated professor to his graduate students, whom he entertained in our home with cocktail parties and poetry readings, at the same time he was an avid hiker and swimmer.

FROM AS FAR BACK as I can remember, my father scared me. Not just his backhand swats. Not just his six-foot-four-inch stature. His melancholy frightened me, his dark thoughtful pauses between words and his high expectations for our articulate brilliance.

Children of academics often grow up isolated inside a bubble of expected intelligence.

I can still hear my dad telling me, "Don't act so silly." Well, it worked. I turned tough and shut down.

SILENCE DOMINATES MOST memories of my father, though. I'd stand at the door of his study and Mother would say, "Let him finish his train of thought." I couldn't figure out why he sat at his desk all day or what he was writing, and what exactly is a train of thought?

Each dusk I fetch him from his study, a converted log cabin by the apple and cherry orchard and chicken coops on the property of our first house. Wood piles lean against the back of his study. I enter his world—"Time for dinner" I announce with caution, and wait, timid in his silence. The quiet swallows me while he scribbles away with a mechanical pencil.

A silence so intimate I'm embarrassed. For something to do and to ease my discomfort, I memorize the room. Old issues of *National Geographic* and the *New Yorker* pile in front of the iron fireplace grate and fill the wide hearth, the stone fireplace always cold. His desk swims with imbalanced stacks of scattered papers and open books, pipe cleaners stained tan with tobacco oil, rancid ashtrays, and a typewriter. None of it makes sense to me. He gazes at me through air thickened from blue-gray tobacco smoke, clears his throat, and, in a voice raspy from not talking all day, says, "Just a sec, Mouse."

He rises from his desk and we head across the backyard into the house for dinner. He never says what he's writing, and I never ask. We talk of other things.

MY FATHER FANCIED himself self-sufficient, almost like a farmer, a contrast to his New England background and his life as a scholar. My father was an East Coast cultural Jew and borderline socialist. His mind disciplined with military-like focus, he rose out of a blue-collar family. He savored aged cheeses and built a cellar for his fine wine collection. He shunned his working-class background in Brockton, shunned his father who worked in a flower shop and played pool in bars. My father felt shame about his roots, but he never lost his Boston accent. In fact he accentuated it the more years he spent away from New England.

He was first in his family to attend college and graduated from Harvard and later Yale for his graduate work. He financed himself through his first years of college by gambling at late-night poker games and with a series of jobs, including weekends as a guard, and he helped put his younger sister through college because he believed women deserved education as much as men.

In back of our first house my father cultivated a small orchard. He'd wander it in season and pick berries, prune trees, and pluck apples. Maybe he wanted to support his family by "living off the grid." My brother reminded me how once our father also grew a short row of corn, one plum tree, and a pear tree. Right within Seattle's city limits we lived with a country feel.

My perfect weekend day was one of silence and solitude. I loved to sprawl in bed and read or sit still and look out a window. Or out back in the garden, I'd poke and roll the thick green slugs before my mother dissolved them with salt. Other times I'd plant myself in front of the poplar tree in our front yard and pop its sticky sap blisters until the whole trunk wept with goop. If I wasn't playing with my neighborhood friend Wendy or hanging around her mother, I'd wander alone from yard to yard up and down our street on the hunt for adventure. Sometimes I stopped to watch other kids play, but then I'd move on, restless.

On some weekends I played around the pond by the house of our next-door neighbors, an elderly couple, Captain Mac and his wife. Captain Mac looked like Captain Kangaroo, white beard and round, rosy-cheeked face often full of smiles. Sometimes Captain Mac sat next to me, both of us silent for hours, while I squatted by their pond and stirred the water lilies with a stick in search of tadpoles and frogs. I'd even bring a sandwich so I could sit longer at the pond's edge. Come pollywog season, I never poked into the water because I wanted to protect their slimy masses and examine the magic of baby frogs as they evolved from their goopy mucus. Science fascinated me then. I couldn't wait for the tadpoles to approach the adult stage, when their legs sprouted and little tails disappeared.

On cool, fall weekends Jonathan and I would rake our long front lawn while Mother weeded her garden. We'd drag our bamboo rakes over the geometry of orange, yellow, and red maple leaves. I'd stay quiet so I could listen to the scratch of the bamboo over the carpet of leaves. Pine needles and leaves blanketed our grassy slopes, and after we'd build high and round mounds of leaves and needles, my brother and I would jump into the piles and flap around in the crunchy leaves. Some would stick in my shoulder-length hair, but I never minded getting dusty and dirty. After enough fun in the leaves, my parents would toss a match onto the piles. The flames pulled me into their power with a dance of heat from leaves and twigs on fire.

MY FATHER AND I shared another routine besides Friday-night fights: jaunts to the Pike Place Market in downtown Seattle on the edge of Puget Sound. We'd shop for our fish and vegetables every Saturday morning, one of the few times I relaxed around him. We'd wander the market stalls, but his pace drove me crazy compared to my quick and nimble ways. He moved with the grace of a ballroom dancer, slow, deliberate, calculated. People strained to hear his gentle public voice, not always his voice at home

We'd watch fishers peddle their fresh catches and farmers and their families sell crisp, fresh vegetables, moist from the washing. The winds off Elliott Bay fused the aroma of fragrant fruit with the essence of fish, all mixed with the steam of French dip juice as its scent sailed from the cafeteria where we ate lunch. I'd never

seen anyone with features resembling mine in my neighborhood
or school, so I felt at home in the market surrounded by Asian and
Mexican farmers and their families. I loved the market for its tough
working-class realness. I wanted to live there, where all the get-up-
and-go of city life merged, to live with the farm families who sold
fruits and vegetables, even though farming didn't fit my middle-
class upbringing.

On our way to the market every weekend, my father and I sometimes drove past the homeless men and women, slouched from either hunger or alcohol and scattered across the grass in Market Park
along the waterfront. On one Saturday trek, we passed a swarm of
men in a food line, who waited in stiff procession in the damp Seattle
chill. My father's eyes revealed grief as he handed a dollar bill to a
man in the park. My father said he believed many of those men tried
to rise above their situation.

"No matter what," my father always told me, "for dignity, for
the challenge of life, do the best at whatever you do. If you work in
the post office, wherever, do your best."

That was one of the few conversations with my father I could
recall from my childhood, though it was more like the one sentence.
My lockdown was so cemented in me then, I recollect few conversations with him or with anyone else.

The street-corner preachers near the Pike Place Market fed my
early fascination with spirituality and ways of worship. Although we
weren't a religious family, I grew up with a broad religious exposure.
My mother was more observant than my father. She sent my brother
and me to Sunday school and lit Sabbath candles, and we said grace
every night in Hebrew and attended synagogue on the Jewish high
holidays. But I grew to understand Judaism more as a culture than
as a religion.

My mother was raised Orthodox. Every spring we visited Minneapolis to celebrate Passover with her five brothers and sisters.
We'd spend a week with a flock of my aunts and uncles who'd

embrace me with abandon. The affectionate racket of a large family gathering put me more at ease than the sedate academic gatherings at home, where my father and his colleagues constructed dense sentences and analyzed every word as if it were a mathematical equation.

Even though I sometimes thought my father an intellectual snob and arrogant academic, I admired his humanity, his instinct to help those in need. Both my parents lived in a strong Judaic tradition of helping others, as in the text from the Talmud: "It is not your job to finish the task, nor are you free to avoid it all together."

I recall a vague memory of my mother's volunteer work as a tutor with a literacy program for inner-city school kids. I can't recall specifics, but I also remember my parents and their friends in day-to-day dialogue about the 1960s civil rights movement. They favored whatever group felt oppressed, and they condemned the privileged, whoever dominated. I admired this until I put something together: *Was that how they viewed me—as a girl in need? Did they adopt me as a social statement, a souvenir of their ultra-liberal principles?*

WHEN I WAS in elementary school, we lived in Rome for one of my father's sabbatical years. One afternoon my mother took me to St. Peter's Basilica and I plunged into a world I'd never seen before, a universe of incense, marble, candles, and stained glass, and of sculpted figures of saints and the Virgin Mary and Jesus.

I arched my back to look up. "Wow!" I whispered to my mother as we stepped through the heavy double doors carved with religious symbols. I imitated the old woman in front of me at the entrance and dipped, then splashed my fingers in the shallow basin of water, a birdbath-shaped bowl the size of a small fountain. When I waved my watery fingers in the outline of a cross over my face and shoulders, my mother swatted my hand away. "Stop that!" she said in a hushed voice. The décor and all of it fed my budding fascination with worship.

ONE SATURDAY, AFTER a jaunt to the Pike Place Market with my father, I charged down our driveway to climb into my secluded galaxy of boards, the tree house I'd built with Wendy in the thick-trunked maple at the bottom of our yard. We'd gathered scrap wood in my garage to pound together nothing more than a platform of plywood and two makeshift windows with a wide plank for a door. We never let our brothers or any other neighborhood kids inside our silent and private haven, and I climbed up there whenever I got a chance, even in Seattle's wind and drizzle. Some days, alone, I lugged up a bag packed with books, blank paper, and colored pencils. In tree heaven, I wrote poems, drew pictures, and illustrated stories I never showed anyone. I collected leaves to decorate the tree-house walls, and Wendy and I rigged a school-locker padlock to lock the door. We formed our own club and kept a notebook of Rules and Creative Ideas. Rules are her idea, and the creative ideas mine.

Perched in my tree-house escape in the sky this particular Saturday, I listen for a few minutes to the wind whisper through the fir treetops, then peek out onto the quiet and steamy street below. It's another day of drizzle. Suddenly I remember Persephone, my puppet from the third-grade school play in Rome, and the flour-water paste and glue our class stirred up to make our puppets.

MY TEACHER ASSIGNED a Greek goddess to each student and we put on a play with our puppets. My puppet, Persephone, goddess of Hades, fit me perfectly. The underworld sat right around the corner from me. My mission in life would be to raise hell.

I kept up my pranks and mischief even on another continent. Before the school year started in Rome, my brother and I spent a summer at camp in Devon by the sea in southwest England while our parents traveled separately, my father in Poland to deliver a lecture and my mother off to sightsee in Edinburgh. We were the only American kids in camp. Mother sent us off with pre-addressed blank postcards which helped me discover a way to reach out to her because writing felt easier than talking. In Devon I bought a miniature pocketknife that, to this day, I still display in my trinket collection. It left me with a scar from a slash across the meaty side of my right hand, sliced in some fancy knife trick of mine that I can't remember.

FLOUR AND WATER, paste and glue. I scramble down my tree house ladder and charge home to grab a bag of flour, then lug it up to my tree. The moment I hit my platform, a sports car rounds the curve at the edge of our neighborhood. The driver steers towards the street below my tree house, and I rip open one corner of the flour bag.

But why pour when I can fling the whole bag?

CHAPTER FIVE

DUETS

THE SPORTS CAR SPEEDS THROUGH THE drizzle on the wet street below and the second its headlights beam against my tree house, I pitch the whole bag of flour out my window.

Victory! Fluffy white powder breaks loose from the bag and sails like an unformed high-speed cloud. The rest of the bag explodes on the hood of the car. Poof! All over the windshield. Science learned from my puppet-making: windshield wipers make a perfect paste with a one-pound bag of flour coated onto wet glass.

But no time to celebrate. The driver slams his brakes and pulls over on the shoulder. Fast as I can scramble, I make it down my tree-house steps and dart across our lawn into my house. I sneak upstairs to my bedroom just in time to overhear a pound at the front door.

My mother's out with Jonathan at a swim meet, so Dad answers the door.

"One of your kids poured flour on my Ferrari," the neighbor's voice booms downstairs.

I'm in for it.

"Deborah! Get down here!" my father shouts. "Now!"

He starts in with, "Why did you . . . ?" and before he finishes his sentence, I blurt, "Haven't been in my tree house all day." I spin around and march back upstairs, no footsteps behind me.

The neighbor storms out. No proof. I'm an unconvicted flour-bag thrower, the bad girl I believe I was born to be. Now I just need to live up to it.

THE WHOLE AFFAIR fed my taste for thrill and adventure, far from my mother's "don't stir things up" way of life. She hated any kind of discord. Even with her fierce will, she restrained her voice like many of the women of her generation. Her ancestors emigrated from the Poland/Lithuania region after World War II, and, like other first-generation Americans, my mother strived to blend in, not to stand out.

My motto, on the other hand: Defy and stir things up.

MOTHER KEPT HER day-to-day life within the rules, but still she wanted a daughter at all costs, a multiracial girl in our still-segregated country, even a daughter who rejected her year after year.

A high-energy drive kept my mother in constant motion. I'd step through the front door after school and find her in a scurry around the house. She'd transfer a vase of flowers in the living room from one end of the teak credenza to the other, then dart over to the other side of the room and restack a pile of books on the coffee table.

Half the time I never knew why she scooted from room to room. An open book on her lap stilled her intensity, or classical music, often after dinner. My mother's insatiable curiosity drove her to constant learning—an art history class at night, lectures about a new archaeological find, tickets to every new museum exhibit, and constant reading. She yearned to earn her master's degree and on several occasions shared her disappointment about how she never finished her thesis on James Joyce's *Ulysses*. "Maybe I'll go back to it someday," she'd say.

Most days after I came home from school, Mother would pause from organizing the kitchen countertop and as soon as I opened the front door, she'd pop two slices of white bread into our stainless-steel toaster.

I had a stress-related eating disorder. Most meals I'd pick at and shred the food with my fork because I knew I couldn't get it down. I wanted to eat and often felt hungry, but the tightness in my gut forced my throat shut. I'd chew and chew my food until it turned to liquid, then pocket the mush inside my cheek to fool my parents.

My eating problem made me a skinny girl, like a bird with stick legs, my arms, long and narrow, dangled from my shoulders. I felt like a hummingbird in a sky full of eagles. Over time, my mother reduced my portions so I could eat a complete meal. One night she set a perfectly round hamburger the size of a marble on my plate, and my all-time favorite, noodles and butter. When I finished my whole dinner, she cheered. But after that night, it was back to picking and poking at my food.

After school, Mother would pull out a jar of her homemade raspberry jam from the refrigerator for my snack, then we'd wait for the bread to turn dark brown and crunchy, the way I liked it. My brother and I often picked raspberries from the patch behind our house. Jonathan ate his plucked right off the bush, while I collected as many as I could in my bucket. I loved to wear the berries like crowns on my fingers. They're still my favorite food, and I still crown my fingers with them. Sometimes we ate the raspberries fresh with cream, then Mother boiled the leftovers for jam.

We sat on kitchen stools with our toast, silent together, and munched on our late-afternoon snack. Our crunches synchronized in a kind of music but if I relaxed a little with our closeness, something took over, like a thorny fist in my gut. I'd march off to the solitude of my room and leave her to sit alone, a piece of half-eaten toast and a dollop of my favorite raspberry jam left on my plate.

The jam knife would clunk into the sink and our ceramic toast plates clink as she'd stack them in the dishwasher. The clatter of her cleanup drove me into guilt that consumed me more and more because deep down I held compassion for Mother. But still, I couldn't help myself.

MY PARENTS LOVED good food and the kitchen buzzed with my mother's cooking. Jonathan and I helped set the table, my father hand washed the dishes and I dried them. My mother taught herself to make fine French sauces and called her sometimes-extravagant preparation for their dinner parties of lamb and couscous "just a little pick up." She prepared gazpacho with watercress in the summer and ratatouille in the fall, and Dad made leek and chicken soup with carrots and bok choy, and French-style omelets with browned butter. He used a special omelet pan that he'd only wipe clean with a damp paper towel, and he'd bark at me if I tried to wash it with dish soap because he thought it would spoil the omelet flavor.

MY MOTHER KEPT a proper appearance. A sturdy, petite woman, always with a ready laugh, she sat with her hands on her lap, ankles crossed, her brown eyes alert and eager with curiosity behind her glasses. She lost herself in reading and gardening, and played the piano and recorder. She made sure she put herself together well, with clip-on earrings and her soft brown hair pulled back. Her Italian-wool tailored suits accentuated her slim waistline, with a silk scarf draped around her neck to highlight her light-olive skin. I wanted a 1960s TV mom like Peggy Lipton in *The Mod Squad*—tall, blonde, and hip. My mother's elegance and reserved demeanor embarrassed me. Even though I yearned for a mother who looked more like me, since I couldn't have that, I wanted one who looked more like other mothers in the neighborhood.

Her soft-spoken voice still lifted with the sharpest wit I've ever known. We shared an in-the-moment intensity but not much else. She always looked complete, a well-wrapped package in under five feet. Although she claimed to be five feet some inches tall, once I grew past the five-foot mark I found out she had stretched the truth.

My mother wore the pain I caused on her soft round face, her brows sometimes bumped together in worry. Most of the time her mouth curved into a slight smile. She'd remind me at least once a day: Try and look interested or happy. Even if I wasn't, she wanted me to look it. Not a chance.

No matter how much I pushed my mother away, she just wouldn't stop trying to reach me. She took a class in "new math" to help me with my advanced homework in elementary school. I excelled in math and spelling, even though I tried not to. Once in a while at dinner my parents quizzed my brother and me on what we learned in school that day. My grade-school report cards often said, "Deborah is timid and withdrawn, and does not work up to her potential," and then, in an attempt at a positive comment, "But her printing is improved." In the column for parents' comments, my mother wrote: "Good. Then there's still hope."

Did she think improved penmanship would help pull me out of my shell?

My brother strived to win in everything, but he wasn't the best speller, and at home during dinner when our parents quizzed us, I would blurt out the correct answer as fast as I could just to better him. Most often, though, something pushed me to want to fail. My parents would tell me I was "intelligent and above average," yet I hated their approval . . . though I sometimes wanted it.

I'VE TAKEN PIANO lessons since age six or seven. Sometimes Mother calls me over to the piano and pats the stool next to her, then opens her music book to my favorite duet, Beethoven's "Moonlight Sonata," with its mysterious and haunting melody. Music stirs some magic inside me, loosens the rubber-band ball in my gut. Mother and I play duets together without talking, and if my fingers dance ahead of hers, she stops and releases the metronome so I can better keep tempo. Then we begin again.

I force myself to focus on the music because if I don't, I lose my place and wander off, hypnotized by the metronome's click click click click. The pressure of my father behind us across the room where he sits and scribbles on a manuscript or reads doesn't help my concentration either.

I love this piano ritual with my mother, and I love her in those moments, love sitting at her side, love how her skillful fingers dance on the keys, her sophisticated perfume wafting around me.

But after one or two pieces, I've had enough. Enough tenderness with her because I can't take it in anything other than small doses. A person needs to open the door, though, for any love to seep in.

Mother wants to play a second tune, even a third, but I can't go on, can't stand the collision in my gut. I can never shake the pictures in my head, the flashes of images in my imagination about women in denim or khaki, behind bars, images induced by television and newspapers of inmates surrounded by stern-faced prison guards with the hollow echo of steel doors slamming in the background.

I tell myself, "A girl born in prison isn't supposed to play Bach or Beethoven duets with her mother." In the middle of a duet, I slide my stool back and take off to my room. Solitude, always my redeemer.

It will take two decades before I tell my parents I had learned about my prison birth.

CHAPTER SIX

FROM THE BACK OF THE BUS

THE SUMMER BEFORE I ENTER SIXTH grade we move to Bellevue, Seattle's latest upscale suburb, into our second house, a contemporary rambler with a fire-engine-red door. It is just months before I find the letter.

On the bus ride home from my first day of school, I'm the first one to board and head to the back for the coveted center seat in the last-row bench. The midafternoon sun beats down on the seat and hot vinyl warms the back of my legs. I settle in and one by one the other kids file into the seats in front of me, all the way down to the last seat behind the driver. Every boy and girl—white and perfect and happy—all smile and bounce and cluster into duos and trios of friends.

The odor of someone's leftover open banana in a lunch bag fills the air, and its fruity scent distracts me from the noisy chatter. Relieved no one sits beside me, I stare out the window, glad the first day of school has ended. Meeting new people is hard for me. I'm not quick to make new friends, always sure that I look odd and kids might tease me about my sometimes earth-yellow skin, sometimes a dark sienna, depending on how much or how little sun I'm under, and racially ambiguous features, different from my classmates' and other kids' in the neighborhood.

My bus stop's one of the first. I peer down the long bus aisle and through the driver's window, our row of mailboxes ahead over the horizon at the top of our lane, a block away. The bus rattles to slow down for my stop and my gut tightens. I hadn't taken the foresight to plan ahead and sit close to the door for a quick exit.

Now I have to walk down the long aisle past the rows of kids, all eyes on me.

I start to stand and the bare skin on the back of my thighs sticks to the rough plastic of the seat. A quick flip of my hand flings my skirt down behind me. My mother had insisted I change out of my jeans for the first day of school.

I brace myself, fingers wrapped on the steel bars above the seat backs to my side, then grip the back of every other seat—left, right, left, right—down the aisle to steady myself from the bounce of the bus and from my panic. Every face turns up to me.

I hate when anyone looks at me for any reason other than when mischief calls my name, and then every bit of attention sends a thrill through me.

I bite the inside of my cheek to gather strength.

What was I thinking? They're looking at me!

Nothing else to do. Keep on. *Go.*

Halfway down the aisle, a girl's voice whispers behind me.

"Nigger," she says in a tone soft enough so the driver won't hear but loud enough to reach my ears. My stomach clenches even more, and the thought flashes through me: I don't even know what I am and you're calling me this?

I never cry in public, but I want to collapse and bawl, run and hide. Gone forever. Instead I pull my back as straight and tall as my four-foot, ten-year-old skinny-girl frame can stretch, bite harder into the inside of my cheek, and hold my breath. Bite, hold breath, freeze. I'll spend twenty-some years in this lockdown position.

Drop your hands, I tell myself. I'm darker than usual from summer days at the beach and need to keep the brown on my arms and hands away from everyone. Just when the bus rattles to its stop, the silence breaks with the whisper from a second girl behind me: "Yeah."

I know it's coming this time, bite deeper into my cheek to prepare.

"Nigger," she says.

I suck in my ribs. *Spin around*, I tell myself like a command, *smack those girls.*

Knock out their every tooth, smash their pointy noses.

But I never turn, never say anything other than inside my head. I hate myself, hate my parents for their whiteness, hate I'm not, and hate not knowing my race. I detest myself. I'm a mishmash like no one else.

By the time the hydraulic door gasps open, my rage and pain have hardened into a deeper lockdown. I run downhill on our quarter-mile lane, past the other houses, past the field of tall dry grasses, and home to the bottom of the lane.

I barge into our house a sweaty mess, my cotton skirt stuck to my thighs, my t-shirt glued to my back, and an ache buried deep in my heart. My mother bustles in the kitchen, wiping the countertops over and over to collect crumbs and spills from her elaborate gourmet preparations.

The bergamot scent of Earl Grey tea lingers in the air and the classical music turned low on the radio soothes me for a moment. I stumble into the kitchen, still out of breath from my dash home. Sponge in hand, my mother turns to me, smiles, and says, "How'd your first day go, pet?"

I'm too frozen for any words to leak out, shredded inside. Can't she tell?

I sit down on the fireplace hearth and press my fingertips into the cool slate edge to keep me from smashing her with my fist. Mother sets down her sponge and buries her hands in the side pockets of her apron.

"How'd it go, dear?"

I force my eyes to meet hers, choke back tears, and in an almost-whisper say, "Kids called me 'nigger' on the bus."

Her eyes widen.

I yearn for her arms around me so I can fall apart against her chest, but I don't want to break down before my mother reaches out first. I wish I could melt into her. Into someone. Anyone. But I can't, don't know how.

She heaves a sigh like I've forced her to talk about my race again. All I want is a hug. Also, all I want is to shove her into the wall.

"But you're just one of us, dear, and we love you," she says. I race down the hall to my room, slam the door behind me, and fall face-first into my pillow and scream into it. Anything to release the venom from my gut before I explode.

I rip into my cotton pillowcase with my teeth and bite the cloth so hard my gums hurt. By the time I'm done, my pillowcase is a shredded pile of strips. I recall my mother coming after me into my room, but I was inconsolable.

I gave up on the idea of ever having a mother. I was on my own. She's one of them, I thought. White, and she won't understand.

CHAPTER SEVEN

BFD

ONE NIGHT AFTER DINNER WHILE I'M helping clear the table, my mother takes my wrist and leads me down the hall towards Jonathan's room.

I'd spent the whole mealtime tapping my empty fork on the edge of my plate.

"I have something of yours to show you," she says.

Now what.

Jonathan's usual chaotic jumble of plastic model-car parts, scissors, scraps of wax paper, glue toothpicks, and decals clutters his room. A clip-on desk lamp flexes low for his close-up detail work with his model kits. It's the opposite of my desk, covered with sheets of paper, pencils, and an assortment of my father's paper cigar rings that he peels off for a special present before he lights up.

Mother unlocks a cedar trunk full of table linens and mothballs tucked way in the back of Jonathan's closet. Her voice is muffled from behind the clothes: "Something to show you."

Why's something for me in Jonathan's closet?

She pulls out a wool toy puppy, four inches long—coarse beige-and-pink yarn wind together. I stare into the toy puppy's button eyes. What's this?

"Here." My mother holds out the toy. Her jaw muscles clench in and out, in and out. "This is yours," she says. "Your birth mother made this. She sent it with you to your first foster home and it followed you here." It's the one time my mother ever mentions my foster care. She doesn't know I've read about it in the letter.

I wrap my fingers around the yarn toy. *Her fingers touched this.*

I try to pull in the pulse of my birth mother through the yarn. She'd wrapped pink thread into a knot to make ears and cut a sliver of pink felt to sew on for a tongue. Its two-inch pink and beige vertical-stripe legs stand strong. The tiny button eyes stare back at me.

"Sent it from where?" I say to my mother's back. She's turned to look out the window.

She lets out a deep breath.

"Where did my mother send it from?"

She pivots to face me and says, "I *am* your mother." Not in anger, but sadness, and it veils her eyes.

"I am your mother," she repeats, her voice soft and unsteady this time.

"I mean my birth mother, sent it from where?" I fight back tears. I can't tell her I've learned about the prison. Just can't. I need her to say it, to tell me I was born in prison, and that the toy comes from there.

"Your birth mother loved you so much she gave you up," my mother says, answering some other question I never asked.

I press the coarse yarn against my cheek and want it to melt into my skin. Then I catch my breath for a moment at the thought of losing my other mother. I'm frozen, until the taste of blood inside my bottom lip snaps me out of it. I've clamped my teeth to hold myself back.

"Gave me up . . . why?"

Silence stirs the room, after which my mother replies with her standard answer. "We love you like you're ours."

"Gave me up . . . from where?" I insist. "Where is she now?"

Silence divides us.

"We'll love you forever, Deborah," my mother says again but by then I've spun out of the room into the hall with the yarn toy.

I lean on the wall outside Jonathan's room and cup the yarn over my nose to inhale its softness, to pull in the wool scent beyond the cedar-chest aroma.

Take me back, I think, and ache inside. Inhale again. I want to inhale my birth mother's scent. Nothing. I try again. Nothing.

I want her in my memory. I miss her but don't know whom I'm missing.

As I bury the tip of my thumb into a thin spot of bared, twisted metal wire under the pink and beige yarn, my mother plucks the toy puppy out of my hands.

"I'll take it now," she says. And she does. She heads back into Jonathan's room with it and I march after her.

"It's mine," I cry out. "Can't I keep my toy?"

Faster than I can grab it, my mother flips up the trunk lid to toss it back inside its coffin of mothballs and table linens, and locks the trunk. "This will stay here until you're older. I just wanted you to see it," she says. Her hands flutter around the clothes hanging in the closet. "In case it helps," she adds.

Helps what? There's so much unspoken between us, I don't have a clue what needs help. She'd attempted another "in case it helps" earlier in the year and offered to buy me a horse. What's she thinking? It's not like I've plastered horse posters all over my room. I never mention horses. My friend Wendy, from our old neighborhood, rode horses, so maybe my mother holds some idea that a horse makes a girl happy.

"That's mine!" I yell, then try to sound cavalier: "I don't care anyway." My toes grip the inside of my socks. I step closer then she leans back against the closet wall and remains silent. We stand face-to-face. "I don't care about you, Mother. Or anyone else." I pause and take a deep breath to prepare for what I'm about to say out loud for the first time. "You're not my mother anyway."

My mother's soft brown eyes hold back tears. I push my face an inch closer to hers and turn my next words into three separate sentences. "I. Hate. You." I storm away, leaving her alone. I feel guilty turning my back on her but hate her more, both at the same time. Rage and guilt replace my confusion, and when I provoke others and roil everything up, it's the only time I feel better.

ONE NIGHT WHILE my parents hosted one of their monthly cocktail parties, I rummaged through the mound of coats and purses piled high on their bed. They expected my brother and me to mingle at their gatherings, but I felt devoured by the conversation of so many adults.

I turned on thief mode as soon as the guests arrived and snuck into my parents' bedroom to swipe a handful of quarters, a pocket comb, another Zippo, and a ballpoint pen. The thieving thrills me more than my mother's declaration about their guests: "They're famous, you know." She reminded me of this after one of my smart-mouth quips about their friends. I can't help that I steal. The secrecy—and even more, the fact I'm never caught—excites me. The tug of guilt afterward gnaws at my insides, but it's not enough to stop me.

Maybe what I stole belonged to Elizabeth Bishop, Ted Roethke, Robert Penn Warren, Mark Strand, Richard Hugo, Gwendolyn Brooks, Robert Lowell, or John Berryman. I didn't care. All friends of my parents and guests in our home at one time or another, the kind of crowd who voted for Dick Gregory for president, the 1960s literati and heavy hitters . . . and I couldn't have cared less.

One night I stole a quarter from Elizabeth Bishop's jacket pocket. No need to rifle through the rest of the coats piled on my parents' bed—I now owned a coin from the queen of poetry.

During a reading tour she visited my parents, but a Pulitzer Prize–winning poet didn't help me feel any more normal. Normal does not look like twenty or so writers with glasses of dry vermouth on the rocks sitting around the living room with your parents and reading their latest creations. The whole thing embarrassed me— the living room readings and the awkward silence right after while everyone sat pondering and staring off into space. Before anyone said even one word, someone in the crowd always coughed during the silence, and others would light up fresh cigarettes.

It was Elizabeth Bishop who led me into a father-daughter talk about homosexuality. It wasn't her plaid shirt that gave it away, but something else I sensed the afternoon I asked my father about her.

He sat me down at the kitchen table with his afternoon tea set up. I still had the stolen quarter clamped in my little hand. "Some women love women, and some men love other men," he said.

It was easy for me to grasp the concept because, after all, every month or so two gay men scampered around our house with feather dusters and aprons strung around their waists to help Mother clean the house. Once in a while she invited them for dinner, and for a short time they joined as part of our family.

I learned a lot that year for just a quarter.

SOME MONTHS AFTER I've read the letter, at the start of seventh grade, I slurp down my half grapefruit for breakfast. I'm in my pajamas instead of all dressed in my usual cords and sweatshirt. A Seattle drizzle spatters the kitchen window.

On the dash back to my bedroom after breakfast, I grab my raincoat from the front door closet. I yank an oversized sweatshirt from under my mattress that I'd tucked under there after an eighth-grade boy gave it to me for his "let's go steady" gift instead of a friendship ring. Nine-inch white-stenciled letters—BFD ("Big Fucking Deal")—stretch across the sweatshirt's maroon front.

There's no way Mother would ever allow me to wear any sweatshirt to school. Just the opposite. She grooms me like I'm an upper-crusty debutante, even though we live mainly on my father's slim English professor salary. We aren't affluent, and my father teaches summer school at Yale or Harvard once in a while for extra money.

My buttoned raincoat hides the smuggled sweatshirt and I make it out of the house, onto the bus, and straight into my classroom with no one noticing. I'm the first to arrive and dart to the front sideline of the room. I lean against the teacher's shoulder-high, open supply cabinet against the wall where she keeps blank paper, boxes of unsharpened pencils, and blue test notebooks.

The multicolored map of the world tacked above the cabinet behind me boosts my courage with its pictures like the photos in our issues of *National Geographic* at home. I belong in the map and the magazines with photographs of people from tropical countries and other continents more than I do in my white family. The map at school gives me a place where I imagine myself, even though I can't say in what country or with what race I might belong. I see myself in the Thai children with my same wide smile and lips. I see my summer-darkened self in the complexion of boys from Samoa. My nose is like that of people from the Philippines. Babies wrapped on their mothers' backs in China wear my eyebrows. I see my own feet in the photos of South American girls, their bare feet brown like mine. Sometimes I even recognize my skin tone in the pictures of light-skinned Africans. I saw myself everywhere in those magazines and maps, and it helped settle the crazy inside me.

THE BELL RINGS. My classmates file in and fill their desks. My heart pounds behind the BFD, and my teacher glares at me for a long second before she leans back against the front of her oak desk, cluttered with stacks of our homework, and presses her palms flat on the wooden edges.

Here goes. I uncross my arms and open my jacket to flash my sweatshirt to the class. The noisy chatter snaps to a stop as if our school chorus conductor had just hit a down stroke. A few kids giggle and some dive their faces toward their desks and pretend to write.

Now what? My timid self slips away.

"Deborah! Go to the office!" my teacher orders me. Her eyes flash.

We lock into a stare down, and a rush of adrenaline kicks into my gut. I shrug. "Go to the office for what? I'm just standing here," I say. I turn my palms upward to the ceiling, fingers spread apart.

Now I'm in control. A sea of eyes shine on me, and we all wait for what's next.

Whose move is it now? Better do something.

I tug at the bottom of my sweatshirt. The creases stretch out and with a flick of my fingertips, I brush off each of the three letters. I sweep away imaginary lint, then trace each letter with my fingertip.

My teacher pulls me by my wrist down the hall into the school office. *I'm in for it now.*

CHAPTER EIGHT

ON THE FAST TRACK

"IT JUST MEANS BELLINGHAM FIRE DEPARTMENT," I say to the principal. "You know, Bellingham."

It's a town north of Seattle.

Adrenaline pumps more fear, more power, more risk into my heart, but I can't stop.

"Not 'big fucking deal,'" I add. "Not what everyone thinks."

Jumping beans somersault inside my stomach. I'm scared but don't dare show it.

The fun's over when the principal calls my mother to tell her to pick me up.

"What's the matter?" the principal asks while we wait. He crosses his arms over his chest. "You have a good home, two parents, what's the problem?"

Guilt sets in. He's right, I have all this.

I want to shout at him, "Don't mess with me!" but I can't. Those jumping beans now pole vault around inside.

Back home, I'm in my room, grounded again. BFD.

More and more I catapult into a well all by myself, a world with my own rules, a world where I'm convinced no one loves me, no matter how much and how often I hear it.

Just because people tell us something doesn't mean we believe it.

SOMETIME AFTER I'M expelled from school, I stash the pocket flashlight I've lifted out of someone's purse under my pillow. I've needed this to read. Up until now, my parents think I'm asleep at night, but instead I sit on a pillow under my bedroom window with the shade cracked, lean against my wall, and prop my *Puffin Book of Verse* on my knees to read under a clear sky and bright moon. The Seattle night clouds limit my midnight reading, but with my new flashlight I can read in the comfort of my bed, buried under the covers. I also write poems and little short stories by the light of the moon and flashlight.

The first time my mother catches me, rather than scold me, she asks, "What's your favorite?" She takes the book and reads from "The Cow," the page where I've folded the corner.

"I love this one, Mother." I love our closeness then, too.

"The cow mainly moos as she chooses to moo / and she chooses to moo as she chooses." She reads the whole poem, all four stanzas, two lines each, twice. Then I ask her to repeat it, over and over several times, the way I read it under my covers.

"Keep the flashlight, Pet," she says and tucks me in. She doesn't recognize that I stole it. My stomach's in a knot from guilt. Even my constant nail biting doesn't help, a habit I carry long past high school.

MANY NIGHTS AS a girl I'd cry at night, imagining my mother gone, dead, far away from me, and yet I hated her close most often, hated her very touch, and at the same time, just the thought of her leaving terrified me. I was scared she'd abandon me like all the rest. Still, I'd wake from nightmares where I pushed Mother off a cliff and she'd tumble a mile down but as soon as my hand pressed into her back, I'd panic and try to save her. Too late. She plummets down, her body in a slow twirl through the air.

I'd wake up guilt-ridden and sweaty, my pillow soaked with tears. I was scared of myself, horrified about the bad in me with these dreams, but also frightened I'd end up without a mother again.

LIFE GETS BETTER with a little chemical help. In seventh grade, I meet an older boy behind the gym after school. He hands me two crystal meth tablets. His eyes widen when I throw my head back, open my mouth, and toss them down.

Within an hour I'm a 500-volt bulb, my every cell alive and at peace for the first time. I need this forever. At last I feel at home in my light-brown-yellow, don't-know-what-race-I-am skin, my adopted-into-a-Jewish-family skin, my prison-born skin. Deep down, though, I still can't stand myself and am filled with hate for everyone. This rage and hate drive me to plan murder. Just in passing, but I give it more than a thought, and one afternoon in school, I sketch a plot with an older boy to off my parents. I plan to snake a hose from the furnace into their bedroom and gas them in the night. *But if I kill them, where will I live?*

Selfishness, not compassion, stops me. I'm afraid I'll go back into foster care even though I'm not conscious of my few years there. It feels like a stigma, whether I got this impression from other kids or from something on television, I don't know. Even today, for most people, foster care brings up images of neglect and unwanted kids even though it's not true.

Mother and Dad, who never learn about my plot, decide my dark moods call for urgent help. And just for me, not for our family, which is what we need.

I'm mute in the cushy leather chairs of psychiatrists and psychologists where I don't utter one word because I'm convinced my parents got it wrong: *they* need help. I find my one power, in silence, the one thing I can control: whether I speak or not. In the one session I remember, maybe the only time I speak to the psychiatrist, I tell him I think my parents might be racist and I talk about the name-calling and bullying I meet—at school, the swim club, at the beach. After he responds, *Well, some people are*, I clam up even more. I need a better answer.

MEANWHILE, THE COUNTRY'S in a civil rights upheaval, and I'm waging my own revolution at home. One day my mother and I argue about whatever daily conflict our relationship brought forth. Again. I don't remember about what. I'm in my senior year of high school at one of Seattle's all-girls Episcopalian prep schools, and it's either this, where my parents send me in ninth grade, or reform school, because I've already been caught stealing from drug stores. My parents must've accepted the fact that the school held chapel assembly every Wednesday, even though the school is nondenominational.

In high school I write my name as "Debi," with a big circle to dot the "i." I also cover social justice issues for the school newspaper: race, and fishing rights for Native Americans in Seattle. The school requires wool uniforms, royal blue skirts, and jackets with top-button-better-be-buttoned white shirts and stand up for the teachers when they enter the classroom. Lunchtime meant formal training in etiquette and meals served in a white-tablecloth dining room. My graduating class consists of twenty girls. Because I stand out in my all-white class, there's no way to disappear into the school crowd and hide my trouble-making.

Every molecule in me is packed with rage. One day at home, I face my mother in the hall outside my bedroom, my body so close to hers, her back presses against the wall. We're the same height by now, but I'm lean and muscular and more athletic than her soft, petite frame, just under five feet. A few summers before, I trained in the butterfly and breast stroke and raced on a swim team, so the workouts shaped me with broad shoulders and strong back muscles.

We're forehead to forehead. Then, right behind my eyes, an electric thread ignites, rearranges my cells inside. It's as if I'm plugged into a high voltage outlet and fueled by seventeen years of fury and adrenaline. I power up to strike and aim my right fist for Mother's face. At the last minute, when my knuckles almost graze her cheekbone, I divert my punch.

My hand pierces the sheetrock wall behind her, my fist a nuclear ball on fire. I can't remember what my mother does other than duck.

I retract my arm from the hole in the wall, my knuckles collapsed. From the nail of my baby finger down to my wrist, the outside half of my hand folds into my palm. The anger, still ablaze in me, blocks the pain at first but my hand soon begins to throb and then turns into a purple-black, mangled mass.

After three days, my mother hands me her car keys to drive myself to the hospital. "Tell them you rough-housed with your brother."

Jonathan's off at college, so that's a flat-out untruth. I've never known my mother to lie, but she would skirt facts to protect the family image. She'd never want to admit my violence and let the world in on our problems. Big problems.

I'd just passed my driver's test but we hadn't been taught how to drive to a hospital with a swollen hand in the lap. My hand and arm throb all the way, my bones already set into a distorted form. I don't feel a thing when the doctor wraps my hand in gauze and then, with what looks like a shiny hammer, rebreaks the bones before he casts my hand. No pain, no more anger, nothing but a frozen inside. I don't even feel alone, though I'm by myself in the hospital.

When head and heart disconnect, the one thing left is total lockdown into a world of only two choices: adapt, or crash and fall. More often it's thought of as fight, flight, or freeze. I'm living in this zone full-time.

SOMETIME AFTER THE disaster of my hand, I downed a handful of aspirin to end it all. I'd had enough, couldn't take it anymore. My weak attempt at suicide failed and I awoke the next morning unscathed. The amount I'd gulped wasn't serious enough to kill me but more about how helpless and hopeless I felt, maxed out and fed up with life. After this, the only road I traveled to kill myself was the self-destructive one—emotional suicide.

LEAVE HOME. That's when I think everything will improve, the day I move out, the very second I step out the door for good. Life will change, I'm sure, and then every bit of rage and confusion and hate will dissolve into nothing but bliss. Grief will flutter away and joy will bounce right in front of me the minute I sail out the front door of my parents' house at last with my bags packed and ready for the good life. And when I turn eighteen, then for sure life will turn golden. When I when I when I . . . What will make me better is always something outside of myself.

Why not college? I head off to Ohio because my mother has friends there who teach in the state and . . . what else can I do? I'm too broke to live on my own for long, and my dad's university job covers our tuition, no matter where we attend.

But it doesn't pan out. My second day on campus, I head to my dorm room after dinner, and my side of the room is empty, all my belongings gone. Come to find out, the resident advisor moved me upstairs to the floor for Black students. The school is unofficially segregated, as so many are even now. When the Black Student Union asks me to join, I figure why not, and attend a few meetings where I make friends right away. The Union is the catchall group for anyone non-white, even though I don't fit into any race categories—I am nothing and everything, neither Hispanic nor Caucasian nor African American nor Asian/Pacific Islander but, rather, some unknown blend.

ADOPTION RESEARCH SURVEYS indicate that not until the 1970s did more than a thousand white families include adopted children of color. My pioneering parents stretched beyond the margins to adopt me. But whenever I asked my mother about my caramel-colored skin and button nose, about the hint of an almond shape to my eyes, she'd tell me she loved me and that I was one of the family. I was too scared to eke out even one word to her in response, to tell her I didn't feel part of anything.

In truth, there was no love big enough to cover the stigma and shame I carried about my prison roots or about my ambiguous racial whatever-ness. By the time my parents adopted me, no love could repair the trauma I'd already lived or the traumas that would follow.

WITHIN WEEKS OF the "eviction" from my dorm room, I round up a few other girls from the BSU and we roam the halls in search of white girls' rooms so we can torch terror into them. We stack newspapers against their doors, then toss a match onto the piles. I'm into fire again, just like I was in elementary school. One college escapade after another, always fueled by cheap Thunderbird pint bottles and opium or weed. College was the first time I smoked opium, and since I'd heard about poets and artists in days past getting all creative on opium highs, I felt sort of artsy instead of druggy. What isn't artsy is the plot I scheme to heist an armored car with a classmate in my economics course. We hunch together in the student union cafeteria over coffee and cigarettes and sketch a detailed diagram to intercept an armored car he knew of that traveled across the plains of central Ohio. But we never get further than an elaborate map and doodle, and a lot of drug highs.

Soon after, in the middle of my freshman year, my parents receive a letter from the dean with instructions that I should "find a college better suited for my needs." I'm asked to leave, and it's perfect, because I'm more than ready to switch majors from liberal arts to street drugs.

I dive into the fast life back in Seattle and travel at two speeds, either invisible or belligerent, both in high gear as I start my slippery slide downhill.

The first time I load a spoon of dope, I go straight to the top of the class and cook up a speedball—heroin and coke. The afternoon I first shoot up, I cinch a belt around my bicep, pull the strap between my teeth, and give my vein a two-finger slap. I register—draw a little blood first before plunging. My palms sweat and my heart races, a horse inside pounding the track to the finish line. It's divine. The coke and heroin flood through me, a chemical orgasm, part birth and part death. It's all a gift, and I'm home!

I'm nineteen and prowl the streets with a boyfriend I've met at some party. Seattle's my city now, not my family's. Jonathan is engaged and getting his MFA in Bloomington, Indiana, and my father's accepted an offer from Johns Hopkins University, so my parents move to Baltimore. While my dad goes more Ivy League, I dive further off the edge.

MY FATHER TAUGHT me smuggling by example on one of his sabbaticals when I was eight. He drove our rented Fiat and approached the Swiss-French border, Mother beside him and my brother and I in the back, where our Dad had stashed his banned Cuban cigars under our seat. Dad pulled over when the border patrol waved him aside.

"Pretend you're sleeping," my dad said. We obeyed my father's commands in the car because if something annoyed him, his backhand swat could reach all the way back to our seats. We learned this early on because he always drove small foreign cars.

At the border, right away my adrenaline surged inside. I didn't understand what it was, other than a feeling I'd grow addicted to: fear and excitement at the same time.

My brother and I slid down in our seats, closed our eyes, and flopped onto one another. The border control waved Dad across, with his two "actor" kids sitting on top of his smuggled cargo.

A DECADE LATER, with three cocaine-filled balloons shoved into my vagina, I turn my body into a drug-smuggling vessel wherever and however I can, and traffic across the border into Canada. My parents—or the cops—certainly wouldn't approve of my methods or cargo. I also carve out the inside of tampons, fill them with plastic-wrapped coke, and push as many as possible inside me to smuggle the snow across the border. If one of those balloons pops or the plastic in the tampons leaks, I'll absorb enough coke to overdose in under a minute.

When Bobby—boyfriend number four—ends up thirty miles outside Seattle in the Monroe Correctional Complex, we go into business. By now, drugs aren't just a lifestyle—they're a living. With a coke-filled balloon stuffed in my mouth, I swagger into the visiting room with a pout, sit down with Bobby and wink. A spark flickers in his eyes. He leans towards me.

CHAPTER NINE

ACT NORMAL

I GRAB BOBBY BY THE BACK OF THE neck and spread his lips open with mine. My tongue thrusts the drug-filled balloon from my mouth to his. When our visit ends, I saunter out of there with the same swagger, proud of myself, relieved I'm not the one who swallows, then needs to dig it out the other end.

We split the money from sales, one of the first times the entrepreneur in me comes alive. Risk and uncertainty: I'm good at living with these feelings now, always ready in my gut to step over the edge, ready for the world to shift and tremble under my feet.

WITH THE TOP down and a trunkload of three suitcases stuffed full of weed and coke, I rip up the fast lane on Highway 101 out of San Diego in my green British convertible MG Midget headed towards Seattle. One of my recent drug deals paid for this sweet machine with seventeen hundred dollars, the cash rubber-banded in stacks of twenties. Two baby-blue suitcases with nine kilos of dope, vacuum-sealed in shrink-wrap, nestle below in a false bottom in the trunk. The leather on the top suitcase is torn from abundant use, so I face it gouge-side-down in the trunk, its raw ripped edges pressed against the dope inside worth thousands of dollars on the street.

My regular setup for hauling dope works every time. I move dope in bulk for Seattle dealers, then drive back down to San Diego to start a deal over again. Sometimes I alternate how I run the stuff to keep my trail unpredictable for the Feds. Either I pack the kilos in my car or ship them through and ride the bus or train along with the cargo. This is before the widespread use of scout dogs to sniff for drugs.

If I travel by bus or train, the insides of my arms come out a mess by the end of the round-trip drug run. In the bathroom stall at the back of a bus, I brace one hip against the outer edge of the stainless-steel sink and struggle to get a needle into my scarred inner arm. Half the time I miss my vein from the shudder of the bus. The sway of a train makes it even harder to hit.

BACK ON HIGHWAY 101, the speedometer clocks eighty miles an hour, James Brown rasps "I Feel Good" on my radio, and the rhythm of the ribbed road rocks underneath.

When Mother gave me these Samsonite cases for my high school graduation, she expected them to pack college essentials—new cords, sweaters, toiletries—for Vassar, Smith, or Radcliffe, where my classmates had enrolled, not kilos of dope and bundles of cash.

I veer around a bend, a roadblock straight ahead of me—two California Highway officers in khakis stand on the roadside. I'm ready for them, though. My third bag covers the goods in the bottom two. I clench my teeth to fortify myself, my jaw already clamped like a vise from too much coke in my veins.

Inside the suitcases, I'd scrunched my clothes around three one-gallon plastic ziplocked bags packed with cocaine. White crosses—aka speed—fill another bag. The third suitcase also shields my cargo in the event of rain. A blow-dry or slow heat at a hundred degrees in the oven always cures damp cash. But who buys soggy weed? Well, me. Dry weed or perfume-spilled-on weed, it doesn't matter. Weak opium or cheap hash, I don't care. Overcut coke or pure-enough-to-kill-you coke or heroin from the dirtiest dealer in town, I'll mainline anything.

One trooper stands feet spread shoulder-width apart. He sweeps his arm into a wide arc of "pull over." Even at a distance, I can see he's the same lean tower of a man as my father's six-foot-four swimmer's build, his legs so long, enough to be able to drive with one knee braced on the steering wheel and tamp his pipe or light a cigar with both hands.

A few car lengths away from The Man, instinct and adrenaline drive me into a panic of survival, a rush with my senses on high alert, my reality altered. It's the same thrill as my childhood jump off the wall.

The midday California heat beats down on my sun-darkened hands—one grips the leather-covered steering wheel and the other yanks the gearstick to downshift, the way my father taught me. He admired Italian sports cars and even on his modest professor's salary, he bought several. I rev my MG from fourth gear to third, to second, then accelerate and shift again. The power of my car hugs the curve of the road.

I whiz by the first state trooper. The second one beckons with his hand and I swerve to the side of the road about twenty feet beyond their roadblock. I glance in my rear-view mirror. The glare from the cops bounces off my mirror. They saunter towards me. One of them forks his hand through his hair.

"Uh-oh," I say to the steering wheel. *Could use a line or two of coke right now.* No time. Just sit. The black-leather seats cook inside the convertible and a queasy heat wave surges through me, even more since my thick black hair absorbs the sun and fries my scalp. A thin trail of sweat swizzles down my temples. *Stay calm.*

"Open your trunk," one of them says. A suspicious half-smile curves on his lips.

My instinct jumps alive with adrenaline. I want to bolt but something stops me. They might shoot me in the back if I run.

My trunk's packed with enough dope to send me down for several consecutive life sentences. It's the late-1970s era of Rockefeller drug laws, and possession of two or more ounces of heroin, cocaine, or marijuana pulls the same penalty as second-degree murder.

Busted or not, no big deal. *Sit tight.*

The trooper leans over my doorframe. I wish I'd tugged the top up earlier.

His pupils dilate while he scans the narrow space behind my seat. I smile. Nothing there because I keep my two-seater pristine. I'd stowed my ten-inch switchblade and .38 revolver under the carpet below my seat. My stack of maps in the back of the glove box conceals my kit: syringe, spoon, rubber strip to tie off, and vial of water.

A Harley-Davidson revs around the bend. A middle-aged woman straddles the machine, her shoulder-length hair pulled back into a ponytail and a few loose strands flap in the wind, free.

Beads of sweat outline the tops of the trooper's eyebrows. Before I step out of my car, I clench my eyelids tight as fists to prepare for the worst, then open them, swing my legs out, and plant my feet on the pavement. I stand firm in my uniform: flip-flops, jeans, and a long-sleeved T-shirt to hide my track marks. I look away when the cop's eyes dart up and down me from head to toe, my one hundred pounds dwarfed by his bulky frame.

They order me again to open the trunk. My rubber flip-flops smack my soles as I mosey at a Sunday-stroll pace to the rear of my car. One trooper hovers on my left, the other steps to my right. I bite the inside of my cheek, a ridge of scars there from so many years of gnaw gnaw gnaw. A hand motions towards my trunk. "Open up." I turn my key in the lock.

Act normal. What's it mean to act normal anyway? What's normal for a nineteen-year-old like me who runs drugs for a living, blueprints burglaries and bank scams, and is the think tank for a small gang of ex-felons? What's normal for anyone? How do we ever gauge if we're in the norm or outside it? Somewhere along the way I learned to compare myself to others. But it's a moving target. Every time I find someone or something "better" than I am, better than I think I am, another "better" comes along.

Pretend the lock's stuck. No. Say you need to pee. Nah, too obvious. Run for it. Nope. Better not. My brain tangles in a debate. Dread pulls my stomach muscles tighter. I force myself to keep my other hand from a dive into my jeans pocket to hide the bulge of the plastic film canister pressed into my thigh. Cocaine fills the case, the snow I need to jolt my eyelids open on the long drive up the coast.

Dizzy from the heat and from the flood of adrenaline, I reconsider: *Bolt!* I calculate the risk and the steepness of the cactus-covered dusty incline to my right. I'd never make it up the hill.

My breath freezes at the bottom of my lungs.

"C'mon," the trooper repeats, his nostrils flared, "open it."

CHAPTER TEN

GNAWED

A SHEER CLIFF PLUNGES INTO THE ocean on my left.

Jump. Soar like you did as a kid, all those leaps out of a tree. But my hunger for thrill slips away—I envision multiple rounds pelted between my shoulder blades.

I flip open the trunk with one hand and dig the other into my pocket. They'll never notice. I grip my fingers around the vial of coke buried in there.

"Just as I thought," the trooper says.

I suck in a reservoir of air to fill my lungs, maybe my last breath of freedom.

He repeats himself before I get a chance to digest the critical consequences of my situation. My heart quakes on the edge of terror. I'm in for it.

"Just as I thought, but we gotta check anyway."

The other trooper slams my trunk closed, then they both turn their backs to me. I draw my spine into a tight rod.

"Not enough room to fit anyone in there," one says.

What?

Their routine completed—a random check for Mexicans smuggled into the United States inside trunks and under seats—the troopers step away from me to approach the next driver.

I jump back into my car and my lungs collapse with relief. "I'm free!" I say out loud.

My gut still tight, I shade my face, use my hand like a shield to hide what just happened, then jam my MG into first gear and hit the road, back on my warpath. Nothing slows me down. It's Deborah against the world.

I REACH FOR a glass of Jim Beam one day and stumble, buckled over from the pain in my gut. I try to straighten but can't. The pain rocks me to the floor where I stay until Diego, my current boyfriend, comes home to our shared apartment and finds me. Diego's a smooth-talking, soft-spoken Mexican American and just out of the joint. I've been a rookie apprentice to his two-time felony crimes. He half-carries me to his car and speeds to the hospital.

We've just returned from one of our drug runs and, an added bonus, a few weeks on the beach in San Miguel, a quaint fishing village in Baja California before tourists invaded. We tooled on down the highway from San Diego across the border in my MG.

OUR FIRST DAY on the beach, I spin out my car into the sand. I forget the science of weight, because as soon as I'm off the damp sand patch near the shoreline, my MG sinks into the dry, dusty sand. Diego gathers a few guys from the beach and they surround the car and pick it up! Then they walk it off the sand. Same happens when we get a flat tire the next day. No tire jack, just a few guys to grip the bumper and lift the rear end while Diego changes the tire.

Our first night in Mexico we both want to sleep on the beach. Diego warns that we'd better put our cash and keys in our jeans' pockets and roll them for a pillow so thieves won't raid our valuables. He grew up in San Diego and spent weekends in Mexico with his family to visit relatives, so he knows things I don't.

It's right after midnight and neither of us needs sleep, neither of us wants it. We peel off our clothes, toss them into the sand, and stand bare, alone on the beach. Forever miles down the sand in all directions to the end of the earth, our naked exposure in open sea air, the galaxy of clear night all around, the risk of public sex and the anxiety of what-if-someone-shows-up, this freedom our foreplay, the start of orgasm before we've even touched.

I lean to kiss him and he pulls me forward. I climb on to wrap my legs around his waist and he falls backward into the sand, me on top. "You okay?" he whispers into the curve of my neck. Often in sex he asks about my needs, not something I find with other men. We kiss and kiss through beach grit and salt air. I straddle him into the late-night heat. The Mexican sun still seeps out of the sand. A coating of beach dust sticks to the sweat on his arms, more inside my thighs. He always comes slowly, and we'd been high all day, smoked Mexican weed and downed shots of Tequila. No sense of time. Hours, it seemed, then he rolls me over and I kneel, grip handfuls of sand. These moments, a night like this, I forget about my past. I forget about the stabs of pain in my stomach.

We fall asleep snuggled together against a dune and wake at dawn, exhausted from the all-night romp and from the drive the day before. We awake aching for more.

After I clear my head, I dive my hands into my jean pockets. All my money's gone. We've been robbed. Diego's jeans are still rolled under his head so at least we have car keys and enough cash to make it through the week.

BACK IN SEATTLE, Diego rushes me into the doctor's office without an appointment. I'm flat-backed on top of the crinkled-white-paper–covered exam table. The doctor ignores my moans. He prods and probes, then shakes his head and schedules me for a barium test.

When he later gives me the test results, he says, "You've developed an advanced ulcer, and over some years."

Some years? I'm not yet nineteen. "Explains the bits of blood when I throw up," I tell the doctor.

He talks about reducing stress, asks a thousand questions, and then frowns when I fold up the paper he's handed me with a list of bland foods to eat. And no alcohol. Nothing on the list about drugs, though.

Oh yeah, I'm stressed. My hair falls out in clumps and quarter-sized bald spots dot my scalp. It's alopecia areata, a temporary stress-related condition. And I've gnawed the inside of my cheek so much it aches from a ridge of scar tissue. I've deteriorated inside and out. But none of it a reason to clean up. Why leave my one friend, my family—drugs. Deep down, though, some glimmer inside knows I'll be better off if I quit. Next Friday, I promise myself. Or the week after. For sure by the end of the month.

The apprentice in me graduates the day one of the guys I run around with gives me a .38 Special with a mother-of-pearl inlaid grip. For the next five or so years, I spiral deeper into drugs and ratchet up my crimes.

My light-brown skin and skinny body, down to the bones from too many drugs and not enough nutrition, lands me honest work one day. A tower of a woman approaches me on the street and places her hand on my arm. It chills me, and I shrug it off.

"Would you be interested in modeling?" she asks.

Me? Modeling? Since childhood, the messages repeat in my head, *You're ugly.*

"I need some ethnic variety in my photo shoots."

I fidget and squirm in the studio, awkward and embarrassed by the photographer's focus on my looks. But I model for a month because of the pay. My rate of $150 for a few hours of work ends up in the hands of drug dealers and in the cash registers of nightclubs and bars along the Seattle waterfront. Despite the regular money, I walk out on a photo shoot one afternoon and never go back—the same way I leave everything and everyone else, even my parents. My solution to everything: stay on the move. No one can abandon me if I leave first.

ARMED ROBBERY, DRUG smuggling by the trunkload, stolen cash cards, and cash-machine schemes fill my days until they lose their challenge and bore me. I'd lost my interest in writing long before. With not enough thrills to content me, I switch to the big time and enroll in bank-teller training school for a two-week crash course. I devour every piece of information and receive straight A's. I've learned all I need to pull off an inside job with my guys.

Two days after the robbery, I throw up one morning right when I wake up, retch and jerk like a rag doll. Dry heaves take over my body. I gag again and again until crimson phlegm swells in my mouth. I cling to the sides of the toilet bowl until my body gives up, then struggle to the bathroom mirror. Burst blood vessels cover my eyes like I'm dripped in pink food coloring. By sunset, still dizzy, I head back out on the street and run into one of my drinking pals, a woman I later find out had a crush on me. We wander down University Way, chitchatting and sharing a cigarette. What happens next changes my life.

HALFWAY DOWN THE boulevard a scrawny white guy flirts with me, unwanted attention, and no matter what I say, he won't stop. The woman I'm with flashes a four-inch buck knife from inside her coat pocket and lurches towards the man. She plunges the blade into his stomach.

I turn to bolt out of there but my feet are glued to the asphalt. The guy clutches his bloody shirtfront, doubles over, and limps across the street. He disappears behind a building.

Never in a million years did I dream I'd cause anyone serious physical harm. My gun, my switchblade, they're just for show. It's not in my makeup to use them on anyone.

I stand there, frozen. A sickness fused with terror rises in my gut at how derailed I've become. Terrified, I decide then and there it's time to ditch the bad life, while I still have a life.

Even before I learn from a friend that the local police and the FBI called her to find me, I flee Seattle. I grab my baby blue suitcases and toss in my leather jacket, a few pairs of Levis, some t-shirts, along with a few other clothes, and—because they boosted my confidence—my switchblade and gun. I fly to Minneapolis, praying that one of my uncles or aunt will take me in.

Uncle Peretz, one of my mother's younger brothers and the one she's closest to, agrees to let me stay with him. He's single, in his sixties, and still calls me his "Little Debbie." But now I'm even littler. He last saw me in my teens when I trained as a competitive swimmer and had a lean, athletic build. By the time I arrive on the run from the cops, he doesn't let on how I've changed: bony and fragile, inside and out. The night I arrive in Minneapolis, my parents call me, relieved to hear that I've surfaced, but not so happy.

Dad bellows through the phone, "The FBI called. They're looking for you."

I shrug. "Yeah, I know."

"Now you'll never get a job!"

My dad slams the receiver, but I don't care. Who needs a job? I need dope.

My uncle hires a lawyer for the investigation of my crimes in Seattle. His kindness warms my heart and hurts at the same time. Weeks and weeks pass, and somehow they never charge me. I spend those months on a white-knuckled ride, my way off drugs and the tremors and cold sweats sweep through my body. I fight back by heavy drinking with my uncle. He hits the bar every night with his friends and I join him to pour the alcohol in me. It's not a beverage—it's anesthesia.

AFTER A YEAR in my uncle's house I moved into my own apartment in Minneapolis. My parents and I were cautious together and protected our fresh start. We never discussed my dark years or my childhood, and we never spoke about my disappearance after I quit college. But they warned me about drinking so much. "Maybe just a glass of water," my mother would say when I'd ask for a third or fourth glass of wine.

EVEN THOUGH MY bouncy brain still fights me, after several more stints at college, I return, still restless inside, still a rebel. I keep far from my parents' field, literature, and earn a degree in economics. Not the best reason to choose a course of study, just to rebel against parents, but it is also because Karl Marx and the study of economy and social justice interest me. How can they not, with the influences of the 1960s and '70s and "Power to the People" so strong in my childhood.

A degree doesn't mean I understand how to settle down, though. Just because I take action to live a more traditional lifestyle doesn't mean the unrest in my spirit settles. My outside and inside don't match. I'm still a mess, still confused, packed with questions about where I'm from, what race I am.

Fact versus memory. If I keep on the move, maybe I can remake facts to create new memories and push the old ones out. Then there won't be any room for old memories to haunt me.

I float through a series of short-term jobs. I staff a group home for court-adjudicated girls, model for print shots occasionally, and work to organize a meals-on-wheels program for seniors.

Along with quitting drugs, I also drop my criminal ways, give up everything cold turkey, more out of fear than from anything else. As the saying goes, I got sick and tired of being sick and tired.

But I'm addicted to another drug, too—high-action adrenaline—and it drives me into a hard-partying crowd of dancers and theater people. Good thing I kept my pool-shark and party talents because I get to use them all over the Minneapolis nightlife and clubs. It's a hazy time in my memory other than weaving through a series of romances and reckless sex with both men and women, where some turn into relationships for a few months, maybe a year or two but not much longer. Why would they? I don't know how to commit. I never let myself join my own family, so a relationship commitment is next to impossible.

Soon after I clean up, my first passion, dance, shoots to the surface and I pick up where I'd left off in my childhood classes. My stocky build is better for modern dance, not ballet, and at last I make my first serious career choice since drug running. Day and night I follow a dream and train to audition for a dance company. I've never before held a dream for myself other than to find out where I'd come from. I follow my dance dream to London, where my parents have moved for another of my father's sabbatical years so he can work on one of his books. I share their flat and stay in the spare bedroom. It's the first time we've lived together since my teens. For a long summer of dance training, when I'm not in the studio, I'm in every small theater I can afford tickets to and attend the Royal Albert Hall summer dance performance series. A dream does everything it's meant to do: gives hope, purpose, and a reason to live.

When a dream means everything, even more than life itself, and then it's gone, that's a problem. Back in Minneapolis after the summer, excitement and nerves bubble in my stomach for a week before an audition. Then one day in the studio, I land from a leap on my right foot, but . . . but I still feel airborne. Something's not right. I know my bare feet have landed on the hardwood floor, I know I'm not in the air, and yet I feel airy. When I look down, my right kneecap has swiveled behind my knee joint. Behind it! I can't believe what I'm looking at—a concave scoop where my kneecap used to be. I also can't believe the pain coursing through my every cell, like nothing I'd ever experienced. I went into shock and remember only that paramedics carried me down the narrow stairs from the top floor of the warehouse studio, into the ambulance, and off to the hospital.

Even with the Demerol IV for pain, nothing can mask the pain when the doctor grips my kneecap and swivels it around front where it belongs. A dislocated knee takes months to heal, and for some reason, mine even longer. I end up in a cast from crotch to ankle for almost ten months. My first night home from the hospital, I ask a friend to bring me a bottle of Jim Beam.

CHAPTER ELEVEN
WHITE-KNUCKLE RIDE

BOOZE AND COCAINE HELP SQUASH THE physical pain and drown the despair about my dream lost. Almost a year imprisoned in a cast and, once again, I'm an addict. It takes a special kind of stamina to chase a dream, and even more to accept its demise. I didn't have it in me to face the crash.

A YEAR LATER, at a house party with empty cases of Freixenet black-bottled champagne strewn about and a glass coffee table covered with coke, I join a dare with a handful of women to take chemical-dependency tests. No reason other than it's a dare, maybe to taunt the system. But no one else follows through except me. The results at the outpatient Hazelden Women's Clinic are not what I wanted to hear. In fact, it disturbs me, but I'm not surprised. They assess me as a full-blown addict.

She gestures for me to sit in the plastic chair beside hers. I'm frozen with fear about the truth. "Deborah, you should check in as soon as possible, in-patient."

I lean back, shake my head, and hide behind my orange bangs. I'm letting the fuchsia side of my hair grow out.

She's wrong.

"I don't think so," I say.

I sling my bag over my shoulder and flounce out of there. Over the next month I traipse around town for tests at five other agencies.

The woman at the second place helps me feel safe with her gentle smile. I like her until she speaks.

"You need treatment, Deborah. Immediately."

I storm out of her office and those of counselors at the other agencies, too, all of whom seem obsessed with treatment. Tendrils of panic and hopelessness try to latch onto my brain but I shake them away. I don't need treatment. I don't need anybody.

But do I want to end up like my prison mom? Anyway, it's not true, I'm not addicted. I can quit any time I want. I'll quit on my own. Even though I've tried before, it's never worked. *I'll quit on Friday,* I'd tell myself. Or, *No drugs and drinking on the weekend.* Or, *Okay, next Tuesday, this is it.*

This time I do quit, on a terror ride with no safety straps and no thrills. Cold turkey sends me into one hundred percent fright. Day one, my body drains of strength. Same on days two and three, and the cold sweats ruin not one set of sheets but also the mattress, which I struggle to turn soaked-side down so I can sleep on dry sheets. On and on for days—cold sweats, nausea, and sometimes a hot, dizzy confusion. I can't tell if it's the alcohol, the coke, the Quaaludes a friend gives me, or the mushrooms another friend brings over to smoke with me. By week two, I continue to retch, my body exhausted as my stomach tries to heal.

After weeks of a white-knuckled hell, I take one last slam of Johnnie Walker Red. It throws me into more tremors, brings me to my knees on the bathroom floor, bent over the toilet . . . and I long for Mother. The memory tears me apart, how she'd thread her fingers through my bangs to wipe them off my fever-hot forehead, her other hand with a cool washcloth pressed against my face. Mother. I hadn't thought much about her tenderness before. I survive the weeks of cold turkey with downed gallons of water, and bags of butterscotch candy, chocolate bars, and chewing gum to relieve my sugar craving, so intense I often spend ten dollars a day on hard candy. But I make it. Clean. And I keep it for a year.

Then one night I go to a party. Music thumps, and I stare across the living room at the gorgeous white mountain of coke on the coffee table. The guests fade from my sight and the vision of white powder grabs me by the solar plexus and drags me over, every nerve on alert. A pile of coke—free for all guests. A little voice warns me from some part of my brain, but I wave it away. My body craves the high. Besides, nothing good happened the year I stayed clean, so what was the point? I've lived more of my life doped up than not. I need the high more than I need to stay clean. This is my destiny, and it takes me to my knees.

By the end of the month, I'm on cocaine drug runs between Minneapolis and New York every other weekend with my roommate, Ann. She's also the woman who seduces me after one of our all-night dance-cocaine-champagne parties.

IN THE MIDDLE of a deep sleep, after everyone has left the house, I awake with her perched on the edge of my bed. *Maybe she wants to talk?* I'm too sleepy to roll over, but I turn for a moment. Her breasts press against the long white t-shirt she wears for a nightgown. She unsnaps the clip in her ponytail and a bundle of blonde brown hair falls over the front of her shoulders. She peels back the covers and crawls in, slides behind me, her body pressed against my back. Her perfume mingled with her sweet sweat washes over me and a surge of warmth swells inside. She reaches around and laces her fingers into mine. "You're a beautiful woman, Deb," she whispers.

It's the start of my entry into a new world. But on our fifth trip to New York, something goes wrong.

A MIDNIGHT RUN for a corned-beef sandwich near Times Square turns into a nightmare. I clutch my neck, struggle to breathe. My throat starts to close. My dope's been cut with something bad.

Ann grabs my arms, then releases me. "Damn. Damn," she says and flags a cab.

The cabbie presses his foot to the floor and my head hits the headrest. We screech alongside a drugstore. Ann springs from the car then pulls me out. I gasp for air. Fear pumps through my blood. *I'm gonna die in the street.*

Someone screams at me. It's Ann. We're outside the drugstore and she's leaned me against the pane glass display window. She rips open a box of Benadryl, opens my mouth between her thumb and forefinger, and throws one capsule down my throat. But I can't swallow. I fight her. Spit it out. She cocks my neck back, forces in another, and seals my lips with her fingers. I swallow, choke on the gel cap but manage to swallow the next one on my own. Soon, my air passages reopen.

Tears stream down my face. "I can't do this anymore," I say.

"Sure you can," Ann says. "You just took a bad hit." She glances at me, the residue of panic flickers in her eyes.

ALMOST EVERYONE ELSE in my world, my peers, has made plans for marriage or lost themselves in relationships or started careers and businesses, signed up on mortgages, and purchased homes. They've invested and saved money, some are now parents. And, emotionally, I'm just twelve years old.

Every other attempt I've made to quit sprouted from a voice inside, a whisper of "I've had it. I'm done." All addicts and alcoholics say this at one time or another to themselves. Whether we listen to this murmur, whether we change and evolve or not, all depends on how much fierce self-honesty we muster. Deep inside, we all meet our own demons, whether we acknowledge them or not. I'd done everything I could to make mine go away and look what had happened. Everything got worse.

FEAR STRIKES ME back home in Minneapolis two days later. Something clicks and I realize I need help. I could've died right on the street. I grab the phone and call a chemical-dependency counselor to arrange a session. One session turns into months of them.

I listen more than talk and answer her intake questions with one-word replies. The counselor suggests that my behavior and escapades have been my way to return to the place I first felt safe: prison. "You've taunted the world to send you back where you first felt love," she says.

It's hard for me to really believe this, but it sounds logical, even though the whole experience lives outside logic. She explains how what looked on the surface like bravado when I was a girl stems from a lack of impulse control, a problem that extended into adulthood because of developmental delays I experienced as an infant. She details how heroin babies go through withdrawal symptoms at birth, and they're bad, she says: convulsions, tremors, fever, sleep abnormalities, diarrhea.

This happened to me? Good thing I don't remember anything!

Just half of babies exposed to heroin are born alive, the counselor says, and those who survive need expert care to deal with the withdrawal and related developmental delays. I've heard child welfare specialists say that something like ten percent of heroin infants have chromosome changes and six percent are born with neuro logical damage. The biggest developmental problem for babies of heroin-addicted women: death. Many don't make it to term.

LIGHT FILTERED THROUGH my mind and the more I engaged in dialogue with the counselors and child development specialists, the more I learned the value of self-reflection. After I read the letter about my birth in prison, my world blew up and life distorted forever. I failed to understand how desperate I'd been to prove my love for the mother I'd lost, my loyalty to her lodged so deep inside me. *No other mother will know my love*, the little-girl me vowed.

I suppose I thought the more I could emulate my birth mother, the less distance would divide us. "They could separate us, but I'd never leave her. I'd love her forever" in what I must have felt as a girl.

From the moment I read the letter about my beginnings, the story of my roots obsessed me, as much about the location of my birth as about the woman who'd birthed me. I needed to learn more, feel more, see more. Know everything.

No matter how much I locked up my prison-birth secret, its poison leaked out, as secrecy does. All the love from my parents couldn't remove the stigma I'd felt, and hiding the secret of my criminal past added to the shame.

"YOU'VE STUNTED YOUR emotional development," the therapist tells me.

"What do you mean 'stunted'?"

"You're two decades behind."

"What?" The word springs out. I take a deep breath. "So what can I do about it?"

She shakes her head. "Drugs so young, using for twenty years, no guarantee you'll catch up."

What if I don't have enough time to catch up? There's not enough of life to re-live twenty years twice over.

MY OTHER ATTEMPTS to quit started because I got sick and tired of being sick and tired, but this time I faced death and, even worse, a possible lifetime sentence to pre-adolescence. All of a sudden this didn't seem so fun. In fact it sounded scary. I felt unsafe in the world with my twelve-year-old emotions in a woman's body. Not that I ever did feel safe, but this was new, and I was facing it all clean, no buffer this time with dope or alcohol. An epiphany didn't hit me the way it does for some people who clean up. Where I was once afraid of living, now I feared dying. On top of this, peers zoomed ahead in their lives full of family, love, and responsibilities, none I knew about much, and I'd trail behind.

ONE AFTERNOON I stagger home from the counselor's office, full of jitters inside and out. Despair dulls my vision. A driver in a Mercedes honks me out of my daze and from almost denting the hood of his car. "You shouldn't be on the road!" he yells out his window.

I agree. I'm back where I left off before I started using. Twelve! Inside a thirty-two-year-old's body. At least this explains why it feels right to date a nineteen-year-old boy, a guy I meet at a dance club.

The veil falls from my altered, drug-free world and exposes raw emotional innocence. Even sex feels like it's my first time. I've been sexually active since a young age—not by choice, not for pleasure, not for experimentation, but because an older boy I knew, someone close to the family and someone I trusted, took advantage of me. And my emotions shut down. The gratification was all his, not mine. Other girls my age ran around the neighborhood, playing on swing sets and slides. They clipped playing cards on the spokes of their bicycle wheels, while my pre-adolescent sexual encounters drove me further into confusion and more shame and secrecy. More reason to barricade myself in emotional isolation, another reason to dump my self-esteem down the drain, to doubt my worth. But born in prison trumped everything.

MY NINETEEN-YEAR-OLD BOY-MAN and I stroll in the summer sun the day after we meet. The wind lifts the front shirttail of his button-down, exposing his sleek stomach and the elastic top of his red boxers above his jean's belt line.

The second we reach my apartment door, we fall into each other.

CHAPTER TWELVE

ONE MORE SECRET

I PULL MY BOY-MAN TOWARD ME, our lips a breath away. I kiss him, but he kisses me back harder. I tug the metal buttons on his Levi's, then wriggle his jeans down around his ankles, his boy–short boxers stretched over his tight buttocks.

He slips his fingers under the elastic lace of my panties and steps out of his jeans. The hair on his legs the same black-as-night as the thick mass of curls on his head. I kiss his chest until he pulls me down on him, and we both squirm out of our clothes. He kisses his way from my shoulders all the way down.

"Do you like what you see?" he asks, kneeling over me. He moistens his lips with his tongue and wraps his fingers around his stuff as it starts to swell.

"Beautiful." The one word to escape with each embrace. And with each rise and fall of the weight of his body on mine, I grasp the newness of everything.

A virgin again, at least in emotion and sensation, I want more and more, never enough. I have years to catch up after shut-down sex in a drugged alcohol stupor, years of one-night stands and week-long flings with boys, men, and a few women, my emotions closed down, unable to share real intimacy beyond brief spurts of lust. I abused substances—I abused my body, too. Even if one of those flings had turned into a passion beyond a few years, I still didn't know how to love. How could I love someone else when I didn't love myself?

My new feelings of lust, not drug or alcohol, bewilder and devour me with this clarity of new pleasure. It's all I want, and I lose track of the physical world outside myself. I lose track of time, of day and night. I don't remember if it is after weeks or months or many months when one day my nineteen-year-old says, "We can do other things besides sex, you know."

Soon after, we break up.

The first months of my clean days, I huddle at home, curl up on the sofa and hug my knees. No one knows I'm getting help. Mother and friends call in the weeks after. I think they just need to check on me, to make sure I haven't moved, haven't taken flight again. I'm scared of who I am and at the same time don't have a clue who I am. Emotional pain clutches at my throat if I need to speak, and when I answer their phone calls, I fight not to cry. I can't leave my apartment. How can I face the outside world?

CHIP, CHIP, CHIP. I break through the walls I've built, the fortress around me. Each chip feels like a slab of concrete crashed to the ground. But clean and sober, I'm still fear-filled, and the fear shields a raw wound. A smidgen of a crevice opens to let in my parents and I take baby steps in a giant's shoes to close the gap and reacquaint myself with them.

Mother invites me for lunch at their new home in Champaign, Illinois, where my dad now teaches at the university after leaving Johns Hopkins. She, Dad, and I sit at the table, and Mother serves noodles and butter.

I look from my mother to my father, then back to my mother, and a volcano shoots into to my lungs and erupts in my stomach. I fight to hold in my words that burn in my throat. Mother and Dad raise their forks. I've held it in so long, now I need to say it, not ask, just blurt it out.

"I read the letter . . . I was born in prison."

Both their forks stop in midair. They look from me, to each other, and back to me.

"But . . . how?" they ask.

I don't answer. Then I ask, "Why didn't you tell me?"

Mother's shoulders sag. "We worried what would happen if you found out."

I almost laugh into my pasta. *Oh, this way worked out so much better*. But I don't say it out loud, afraid my sarcasm will hurt them.

Mother manages a smile, and we say no more. A heaviness lifts from me. At last we've cracked the door to The Big Secret. At least she gave me an answer. Even if I didn't agree with all their intentions, they meant well but didn't know any better, and these days, families with transracial adoption receive more resources. I'd blamed my parents for what they didn't know, their lack of information.

AFTER THE BIG breakthrough visit to Illinois, Mother and I fly back together to Minneapolis for her to hang out with me for a long weekend. We museum hop the first day, then after lunch at the Institute of Arts, we charge up the granite stairs to the top floor and stand transfixed by *Veiled Lady*, a marble sculpture from the 1800s. We both love her crisp features and white veil sculpted in the illusion of gauzy, translucent silk to cover her face. This trompe l'oeil technique, or "trick the eye," speaks to me about illusions and what we hide from ourselves.

Side by side in front of *Veiled Lady*, Mother reaches for my hand, and my breath catches. My old pattern always forced me to cringe, pull away and reject her. But I've kicked other habits . . . I slow my breathing and then rest my palm against hers. I'm still a little girl inside, still cautious, but a new twelve-year-old. Mother and I hold hands and it's the first time I remember when mine melts into hers.

A sigh ripples throughout the whole family across several generations when Mother and I at last nestle into our new and bonded relationship. Everyone had hoped all along that we'd one day love each other as daughter and mother, and at last we made it.

I never let Mother close to me, either physically or emotionally. She didn't stand a chance against my fierce loyalty to my biological mother. No one did. But Mother was the one with the stamina to wait for me. Some things just take time. Decades even. I've never met another person with my mother's patience.

EVERY TRIP MOTHER makes to Minneapolis to stay with me, we hop in my car to view *Veiled Lady*. Visit by visit, the tightness inside me begins to release. When I trek to Illinois, we swim laps in my parents' backyard pool, and Mother and I play piano together.

Around Dad, I still feel cautious even though he's stopped his backhand swats at me. Just his presence in the room drives me to retreat into my shell because his intense intellectual energy and potential for outbreaks of rage frighten me. At the same time, I'm drawn to his gentle compassionate side and quirky wit. I live on edge around him, but now that I'm clean I grow to love his warmth when it shows up.

Mother, my white-haired and wrinkled and now seventy-four-year-old mother, her eyes glow, her heart pours out to me. She's waited so long for the daughter she's always wanted. We both open up and receive and return precious love. At last, I have a mama. At last I'm daughter to the woman who believed in me even when I didn't believe in myself.

THERE'S NO TELLING what's behind a wall after it crumbles and crashes. Now that I've stepped back from the fight against myself, family, and the world, my love for reading, for poetry and short stories, reignites. Soon after I start writing again, I win the American Association of University Women's poetry award, and my parents celebrate with me. Followed by a series of grant awards and honors for short stories, I take on my first full-time job, as a freelance writer-in-residence in Minneapolis public schools. But still something digs at my gut, like a thin sliver of glass stuck in your finger that you can't pluck out.

Despite my new bond with Mother, a piece of me still craves to find out more about my prison mom. After a little investigating, I find a search agency that's in the business of uniting biological families and adoptees.

"I'm pretty confident we'll find her," the "search angel" says.

My heart somersaults. *Would I look like her? What would she think of me?* For weeks, my mind ping-pongs questions and they fling me from excitement to fear and back again.

The agency calls a month later. "We have news for you."

My breath catches in my throat and the hairs on my skin spring up like miniature soldiers. *Okay, breathe.* I've waited forever to reach this point, this close. Then . . .

"I'm afraid your mother is dead."

Dead. I roll the letters around, over and over. The word taunts me. All these years, so much pain and chaos, and lost time, so much brokenness and yearning. And she's dead.

"Deborah, you okay?"

I nod into the phone.

"But we found a half-brother. You both have the same mom."

A brother. A link to my birth mom.

"I've got his phone number. Got a pen?"

I scramble for a pen, drop it, and grab it again. I hang up and stare at my brother's phone number. My mother's dead. So is my life-long dream to meet her. I yearn for a needle in my arm to take away the fear, the sorrow. A slam down of Johnnie Walker Red. Anything. I draw on everything in me not to score some dope.

Instead, I exhale, pick up the receiver, and dial. My brother, Nick, picks up on the second ring. In a few weeks, I'm on a flight back to Seattle to meet my birth family. Besides Nick, who's about ten years older, in his forties, I'm met with open arms by aunts, uncles, and cousins. All this time we've lived in the same area! They're just north of Seattle. They welcome me as if I've returned from a long summer away at camp.

Nick and I had different fathers, and it shows. He's half Irish. And talk about shocked, he'd thought he was an only child. Our mother never told him he had a sister, never told him when she was sentenced that she was pregnant. For most of her life she was in and out of, first, reform schools, then jails and prisons, and almost always on drug-related charges. It's the same case today, too. According to the Bureau of Justice, more than half of prisoners, both men and women, are incarcerated for drug-related crimes.

One of our aunts raised Nick, and he was used to our mother being in and out of prison. While I grew up without her, he grew up with her broken promises.

Secret on secret, but this time I'm the family secret.

Within moments of our embrace, Nick says, "Your voice, your gestures, you move your head like our mother." His words pump a new confidence inside me: I am her, of her. And then the connection hits reality. My addictions were part of her too, and maybe the thrill-seeking.

Nick leads me into the house and perches next to me on the sofa. He reaches for a photo album and places it on my lap. "Our mom's."

My stomach flips.

"Her brother, our Uncle Tom, kept it hidden from me until you called." Tears brim in his eyes. I blink back my own.

He leans into me, wraps an arm around my back, and opens the album. I gasp at the first page.

CHAPTER THIRTEEN

WEEPING MOTHER

INSIDE, RIGHT OFF THE BLACK-CONSTRUCTION-PAPER photo album page, a lock of my baby hair and my baby picture stare at me. My mother kept a lock of my hair! I stroke it with my forefinger and swear I sense her love seep into me. It takes a while before I can turn the page, then I move on through page after page of photos of her, and a sense of belonging fills me to the core. I want to dive into those photos and live inside them with her.

By the time I reach the end of her photo album, one more puzzle piece slides into place—I have the hands of my bio mom, her smile, the fire in her black eyes. At last I look like someone else. But I notice differences, too. My eyes more almond shaped, my nose smaller and broader, my coloring darker. Still, questions burn into me: "What else am I?" "What about the other half?" My birth mother was Greek, I learn, but I'm clearly a blend of more. But what?

Nick steps away to answer the doorbell and brings an olive-skinned sixty-something woman about my height into the room. "This is our cousin, Sophie."

Excitement of this union of new family bursts into hugs and smiles and more family, more connections with Martha, my prison mom, aka Margo, as I learn she liked to be called.

"I needed to see you," Sophie says, "tell you about your mom's plan." She smiles. "Something your mother yearned for her whole life." She looks from me to my brother and back to me.

I want to pry every bit of information out of her, my core desperate to know everything.

"Right before she died," Sophie says, "your mother stood at the nursery window in the hospital, stared at the babies. She intended to hire a detective to find you soon as she felt better."

The thought of her at the nursery window with hopes to find me almost topples me over, dizzy from sadness. It wasn't just me, one-sided. She'd yearned to meet me and we'd missed each other. I can't bear the crack in my heart. "At least she wasn't in prison the day she died," I say.

My mother died from throat cancer, I learned, but she thought she'd be able to kick it and leave the hospital.

Another cousin arrives, Madlyn, dark-haired and lean like me. She sits and clasps my hand in both of hers. "Your name, Madlyn Mary, it's a family name."

An image of Mother springs into my mind. I laugh. "My adoptive parents are Jewish," I say. "Madlyn Mary, not quite a Jewish girl's name."

IT WAS A whirlwind of a weekend. I returned to Minneapolis carrying memories and stories from my new family and mementos of my bio mom. They gave me a silk scarf of hers, her diamond ring, and an engraved wooden cross, all nested in my jewelry box to this day.

A last patch of wholeness filled me after meeting my birth family, and the walls I constructed around myself began to crumble. I needed to do something as soon as I returned home. I dragged my suitcase from the back of my bedroom closet, opened it, and pulled out my pistol. I ran my fingers over the barrel. I hadn't used it except to threaten people in a few heists, over a decade ago. It was time to let go of my past even more.

The gun's weight in my hands haunted me. What would've happened if I'd continued on my old path, my life of crime, drugs, and self-destruction? Out of curiosity, not with a plan to use it, I checked the chamber: frozen. I rose to my feet, hurried outside to the dumpster, and tossed the gun inside. A piece of my dark past I was glad to discard.

For many years, none of us knew what to do after the reunion. We exchanged holiday cards and occasional letters at first, and I attended a cousin's wedding. But I didn't call often because I didn't know what to say. Big life changes take time to sink in and find their design.

After a while, Nick and I began to call and text one another, and now we've slid into a family pattern of our own.

SOMETHING'S STILL RAW in me even after all the healing I've forged through. I'm still tender like an over-ripe raspberry balanced on a single-edge razor blade that's going to get sliced no matter which way it rolls. And that's me, shaky and raw, my insides scrambled and carved up.

I'm clean, I've straightened up, I've even begun to work out and use my body to rewire my brain. Most days I'm in the gym for a few hours, on my way to better and better health. Still, something claws at me. I've at last connected with my adoptive family, above all with Mother. I've met my birth family, and I know a little more about my birth mom, and still . . .

Two questions haunt me: "What am I?" "What race or races am I?" I'm sick of checking the Other box. Sick of my answer, *I don't know*, when people ask what I am. As a teen when I tired of people asking me my race, I'd respond, "Hundred-yard dash." Besides this play on words, the answer gave me my own race to belong. Wherever I go, people think I'm one of them. I'm sick of this too. By fitting in too many places, I feel like I fit in nowhere.

And then there's the prison. How is it possible anyone is born in prison? Even though I've grown to accept the fact, sometimes it still doesn't feel real.

Even when I try to ignore and push away my uncertainty about race and about my birthplace, a feeling of isolation floods me. Too often I feel alone in my story because I've never met anyone with a story quite like mine, and often I still forget.

After I meet my birth family, I bury my lingering uncertainties with work. Always an entrepreneur, an idea person, I continue a freelance life and work as a writer-in-residence in public schools. A million ideas swirl in my head and a mountain of energy burns and bring me back to my true creative nature. I also dabble in real estate investment and buy and sell a few commercial properties.

The risk and adventure I craved during my years on the streets shows up in my entrepreneurial work. It takes risk to shape an idea and implement it into a business, the same risk I knew on the streets. It takes guts and courage to believe in your own ideas and bring them into the world. I'm best at the idea part and not the best at the business end of things.

But I plow the most energy into my relationship with Mother.

ONE DAY SHE CALLED. Frantic, she asked, "Can you meet me at the Mayo Clinic?"

"Why? What's going on?"

"I've been diagnosed with . . ."

A pause gripped around my lungs and cut off my breath.

I heard her breath catch.

"I've got ovarian cancer."

"Oh, Mother." I stumbled backward and somehow managed to stop the phone before it slipped from my hand. It couldn't be. Mother never got sick. A strong, healthy, seventy-something woman, she swam laps, gardened, snowshoed, worked out in aerobics classes every week.

She and my father drove from Chicago and I met her at Mayo, about an hour south of Minneapolis. While doctors explored whether her cancer was advanced or not, I stayed with them for three weeks in the hotel, weeks both desolate and precious, which gave us both a gift: time together and the intimacy to grow closer.

We'd lost two decades and needed to make up for all the years of my childhood when I pushed her away.

Later in the hospital, I pulled a chair to the side of her bed, held her hand, and stroked her pale skin. She turned to me and smiled. "You know, we wanted to adopt more children, at least a third child, but you were so troubled and difficult, we couldn't handle more."

Oh, thanks for sharing, but not really. Did I need to know I prevented a piece of her dream, her vision for a family of three kids? Then my heart swelled—she's shared this secret with me, trusted me even after all those years of broken trust. But soon the good feeling shriveled from shame. What other problems did I cause? What achievements did I prevent in her life?

After week seven Mother headed back to Illinois to begin chemo. I called her two or three times a day. Month after month after month I flew in to visit and bring her fluffy socks, bathrobes, magazines, all I could to comfort her. What gave the most comfort showed by the glisten in her eye, the smile on her full lips—her daughter sitting at her side.

She waited these thirty years for her daughter. A mother's endurance can hold a fierce love, even if the link is not by birth. At last we both embraced the bond, but saddest of all, it was towards the end of her life.

I BELIEVE CERTAIN things happen for a reason, even if the reason is obscure or painful. After twenty years of letters to plea for information to the prison where my birth mother was sentenced, where I was born, the warden calls and invites me to visit the prison. The gates open with a warm welcome for a private tour. The timing couldn't have been worse: Mother's on her deathbed.

Prison is my birth country, a land I yearn to visit the way people adopted from Korea, India, China, the Philippines, various African nations, and every other country abroad yearn to visit the places of their birth. Most people at least hold a curiosity about their roots. Even non-adopted people seek their homeland.

I'm headed home. My mother country, prison.

Even though I've been raised with middle-class opportunities, I've felt exiled and paralyzed, deprived of my homeland. At last I'm headed to my motherland, a location up until now I've only imagined, a place elusive and bizarre but never real. I'm about to replace the impressions of prison promoted by television, movies, and public opinion with my own personal and private images. As difficult as it might feel for others to understand, I'm about to enter a world I'd always imagined as my place of comfort, a nest. While this contradicts the usual association with the word "prison," a part of me connects the word and the place with love and safety. For any adult, we know it's not true. For me as an infant, though, prison was the first place I felt loved.

It's taken me into my thirties to exchange a trunkload of dope for a BA in economics, a clean record, and in my garage, two collector's Vespa scooters alongside a classic MGB (not the same one from my drug runs on Highway 101). Legitimate money from several businesses I've founded fills my bank account, although not often with much to spare beyond living expenses.

ALDERSON NESTLES IN the Appalachian Mountains. Muddy Creek and Wolf Creek run nearby, streams named like characters in my life story. Morning mists cover the prison each dawn with a shroud of fog. Hummingbirds dart through willow trees and hover above fields of lobelia. In Seattle, Mother would attract hummingbirds to our garden with tubes of honey dangled outside the kitchen window. "Legend links this little bird to a miracle," she'd tell me, "the miracle of joyful living from life's difficult circumstances."

The night before my prison tour I stay a mile away at the Riverview Motel, its address: Rural Route 2, Box 0. My headlights hit the motel sign: *We Hardly Exist*. Exactly how I'd felt for most of my life.

The Riverview connects to the town gas station, which shares a wall with the grocery store, its shelves lined with cans of Spam, big jars of pickles, pink eggs in a jar, pickled pigs feet and snouts, sardines, potted meat, and Yoo-hoo chocolate soda. Not quite the gourmet delis in Seattle where Mother used to fill her grocery basket with capers, virgin olive oil, and Bibb lettuce.

Four miles outside the prison gates, set back from a hairpin turn on Highway 21, rounded granite forms itself into a five-foot-high hunched stone. Weeping Mother, the locals call her, stumped like a pestle without its mortar. She stands isolated, attentive in the field.

I approach the prison gates, my legs in a wobble. Clouds dip in and out of the horizon then open to blue sky. Two federal officers dressed in dark-blue uniforms eye me through the wrought-iron bars. One officer nods to her colleague, who opens the gate. I wonder if the prison kept my earlier documents, the letters I've written year after year, the times I appealed for facts about my birth, for details about my prison mom. Always I'd close my letters with one question: *Can you tell me what race I am?*

"This way," one officer says.

She flanks me as we walk to the main prison building, a red-brick, two-story rectangle. *Is this what it looked like when they transferred my mom here?* Her sentence began in the Medical Center in Lexington, Kentucky, then called the US Narcotics Farm, where the rehabilitation method for addicts and psychiatric inmates was known as the "Lexington Cure," as if addiction could be cured rather than treated as a disease. They transferred her to this prison when the authorities learned she was pregnant. I've never understood why they didn't know she was pregnant when the court sentenced her.

Footsteps crunch behind me. I shoot a glance over my shoulder. The tall officer follows us a few paces behind. A horn blast pierces the compound and makes me jump. The officer at my side says, "Three o'clock inmate count." The inmates race to their cottages.

I'm back where I matter.

The officers escort me to the administration building across the compound. Six two-story brick colonial buildings sprawl around the campus-like prison in a semicircle.

An inmate sweeps the entryway and her movements mesmerize me. Did my mom stand here on these steps once, hunched over a broom? I wonder. Or did they relieve her of any work duty because she was pregnant?

Lost in my thoughts, I stumble and bump into an officer at the top of the stairs at the entrance. Inside, another inmate in a t-shirt with her inmate number inked on the front lugs a string mop and swabs the faded tile floor like a sailor.

We reach the control center and the guard stops. "Wait here."

I nod, my feet glued to the floor. Three officers surround me. The buzz of foot traffic casts a spell on me. Five administrators line up to slide their clip-on plastic badges into a steel cradle embedded in a steel ledge framed by a bubble of bulletproof glass around the control room. Inside, three guards inspect name-stamped aluminum tokens in exchange for badges, keys, memos, radios, and authority. Other guards behind the glass monitor moments of freedom and stare at a row of closed-circuit TV sets.

Two correction officers break the spell with their laughter at an inside joke.

A five-minute wait turns into twenty minutes while I wait for someone to process me through security. At last an officer waves me into a room. Inside, behind a metal desk, another officer tilts back on his chair and gestures for me to sit opposite him. He pushes a stack of forms across the desk. "Fill these in."

I finish the forms just as a female officer bursts into the room. "Prints," she says and gestures with her head towards the door.

I shove the stack of papers back across the desk and follow her down the hall to a room where a different officer presses and rolls my fingertips onto a black ink cushion.

So this is what my mom went through.

"We need two sets," the officer says, "one for the FBI, one for the BOP."

"Doesn't the Bureau of Prisons have enough on file about me?" I ask, not expecting an answer.

"Other hand."

Afterward, I scrub in the sink with their grease remover, but a faded shadow of ink still embeds in my fingertips. I lick my thumbs and rub them over the other fingers but the stains don't lift.

"This way," the officer says. She opens the front door to the grass compound on the other side. On the way out I fight to return the guards' generous smiles and instead wave my hand like a schoolgirl.

In secret, I'd always loved the word *prison* and every word related to my first home. I'd imagined them all when I was a girl: *dungeon, lockup, the joint, the pen, penal institution, reformatory, detention center, the can, the slammer, the clink.*

My heart skips a beat. At last, my feet march on the prison compound: left, right, left, right. I can't believe I'm here, where I screamed the place down 24/7, spat out milk because my body craved her drug, the dope I'd grown with, plagued by withdrawal—vomiting and diarrhea. Why did Lady Luck grant me life? Or was this my fate, my destiny to survive my drug-exposed birth but then return here? Or was it more than luck?

Like a dandelion puff on a breeze, I fly off above the prison in a distortion of time and space, my cells in a dance. Did my mom's mind flip like this too? I fight emotional lockdown. I've no place inside where any of this fits.

I'm at the threshold of something I've imagined my whole life.

"Let's begin on the compound," the officer says.

CHAPTER FOURTEEN

FULL CIRCLE

"OUR MOST FAMOUS HISTORICAL INMATES INCLUDE Billie Holiday, Tokyo Rose, Squeaky Fromme," the officer notes as we cross the prison complex. She launches into an impromptu history of the place. "No metal fences surround the camp, just a hundred rural acres, a natural barrier of rolling West Virginia hills."

Come back, I tell myself. I can't ground my body in the present. *Come back*. I need to focus. I want—need—to savor my return home, remember every second of what took a lifetime to find.

"Are you okay?" the officer asks.

I shut my eyelids for a minute, desperate to shake off the sensation and keep this weirdness to myself.

But the time distortion wins. We're now in an empty basement room in another building the same compact size as the Riverview Gas Station down the hill. Déjà vu flashes through me, along with a dizzy spell, and sensory memory kicks in like a full orchestra inside. About to pass out, I press the palm of my hand against the door to brace myself. Faded-green paint chips tumble to the ground from the pressure of my hand.

"This paint," the officer says, "it's the same since your birth here, never painted, same since the prison first opened. This is where we used to release sheets of paper for letters and envelopes to prisoners. Your mom must've carried you in here every day."

The air tastes like warmed mold. I hang on to the officer's words, inhale the prison, this landscape I'd shared with my mom, a bond of perfection I'd created in my mind. But for how long?

My breath races faster. Don't let her see. I try to hide the heave of my shoulders so the officer won't notice them rise and fall. I don't want anyone to witness my feelings yet, for sure not a stranger, an authority figure. Fast-paced everything: heartbeatbreathvision, one blur of sensation. I'm like a trapped animal set free.

"Up there," the officer points to the ceiling, its faded white paint now chipped and speckled. "That's the chapel. Service every Wednesday and Sunday. You might have attended church with your mom. They baptized you here I'm sure."

Baptized? I was raised in a Jewish family and I've been baptized!

Jewish mysticism speaks about two powerful muscles in the brain: memory and imagination. But what about the pocket in between, where memory reaches out to imagination but can't quite connect? All my life I stored my prison-birth secret in this pocket to hide it from myself and from the world.

The dank, chipped-paint basement beneath the prison chapel pitches me into this brain space. Silence all around except in my head, I'm transplanted back in time, to a Baptist service and the reverberations of a chapel full of women. Hands clap, women sing spirituals, feet stomp. I'm desperate—is this my imagination or a memory revived?

We cross the compound again, towards another corner of the prison.

Then something doesn't fit. *What about all those times they sent her to solitary confinement? My prison mom couldn't have kept me with her in the Hole. Where did I go? Who took care of me in those weeks and weeks and weeks, on the many occasions she sat in isolation?*

I ask the officer, and she answers almost before I finish my sentence, as if I'd just asked her the time of day: "Oh, you went to the Hole with her."

What on earth does a baby do in the Hole week after week? Isolated in what some call the Box or the Pit, secluded behind four walls. What does anyone do but flip out in the Hole, where psychologists research the breaking point of our human mind, where incarcerated women and men go mad because sensory deprivation can drive a human being to chew the veins in her wrist in a suicide attempt to end the insanity.

Some inmates in the Hole holler and scream all day and night. Others throw feces out their cell doors. Some pump out a thousand push-ups a day to drive themselves to a different breaking point. Others rock back and forth under a blanket for a year or more in this space with just enough room for a bed, sink, and toilet, and no television or radio, just the scream of your own voice and the open-and-slam of doors and the cry of insanity from others in the same isolation.

Doubt and distress and torment live in the Hole, along with terror, frustration, boredom, rage, and depression.

For my prison mom and me, though, all I imagine is an oasis of peace. Maybe she had a box of Kotex, some paper and a pen, maybe a Bible. The guards must have brought diapers and blankets for me. I suppose I was her angel of glory in a dreary place where she created a sanctuary out of chaos, where we cuddled and she could count my toes and sing silly songs. Maybe going crazy was not an option for her with me at her side. Maybe the isolation was worth it for her.

I still can't metabolize the fact: I lived in the Hole at a time when most infants rock in cradles, visit grandma, bathe in a sink, and get diapered with baby powder. A time in a baby's life for the sweet sound of "Awww" instead of the clang of a food slot and the yell "Chow time!"

Me with my prison mom in the Hole, just the two of us with everyone on the outside watching our outlines. How bad can this be, though? But instead of fear, I force myself to lean into the unanswered questions of what I can't reconcile. I use this new-found discipline so the uncertainty won't eat me alive and drive me crazy.

GRASS AND CONCRETE layer the compound, but the ground has fallen away in this out-of-body drift. My feet float, air-filled dumplings. Another space jump. I'm on the first floor of a two-story brick co-lonial, this one deserted. The afternoon sun slants through an open door into the hallway. We enter and the officer says, "Your mother delivered you in here."

My head's about to explode from emotional overload and from the humid ninety-five-degree West Virginia August heat. The of-ficer's shoes scuff on the tile and echo across the empty hospital room. I jump. She looks at me, waits for questions. At last I stand in the place of answers but I can't eke out any words. *Was it a difficult birth?* I want to know but I'm silent, mute. *Did my mom pant hard for air?* Part of me, desperate to ask, tries to speak, but another part, all I can manage, is a long draw of air. I'm speechless. I suck in a breath, imagine the scent of my mom's birth sweat from more than thirty years ago.

Another time distortion sweeps me up and I imagine a collective thump of my heart with my prison mom's, as if we're together again in this barred hospital room we shared. Joy floods through me and I blink back the tears. No way do I want this officer to see me cry.

We inch across the compound and the officer leads me to Cot-tage C, two floors of long rows of rooms on either side of a hallway. I try to make small talk with the officer, but I feel transported back into my preverbal life in prison. My senses on fire, my cells alive, and I'm without words.

She points to an open door on my left at the end of the first-floor hall. For a second, I wonder why we approach this door: C7. Then it hits me. It's the cell I shared with my mom.

The officer and floor guards hang back. I approach the door. My breath catches. Air traps in a cave at the bottom of my lungs.

The last place she held me. She loved me in this room. I loved her here.

For the first time I think of her pain and loss, not just mine.

I try to step into the room but my boots glue to the tile. I can't lift a foot. I lean forward, bent at my waist to scan the room for a second. I spin back into the hall and press my back against the wall. My breath still stuck, my head about to explode again.

I turn and step into the door threshold, try to enter this five-by-eight-foot room, my first home. There's just enough space for a table, chair, and bed. I stand in the doorway and the cell soothes me like a scene in the dollhouse I played with as a girl. My home, this cell. I slept in here, ate, crawled around. My body melts, relaxes into a comfort like nowhere else before.

Go in, step in there.

My skin starts to itch, panic stirs in my gut. I tell myself, *Go!*

I shake my head. I can't. I blank out, then soar back in time to the moment in the middle of the night when someone snatched me from my mom's bed.

Part of me yearns to dive onto the coarse tungsten-colored blanket, bury my face in the bed, and cry. I don't, but now I wish I had. I missed my chance to turn around and wave bye.

Was there nothing to keep my prison mom clean, the way I found motivation? Why didn't she fight to stay out of prison, to stay clean from addiction, to begin a new life? Why couldn't she do what I did? Why didn't she? Couldn't she see any choices or chances? What if she'd quit drugs, stayed out of prison so she could look for me, find me, stay with me?

She didn't get the chance to read any of the poems and stories I wrote as a kid or sit in the front row at my dance and piano recitals. She missed the times I fell into hell, and she couldn't teach me her street savvy, how to run from the cops or hunt the streets for the dealer who passed me bad dope. She wasn't around when I passed out drunk or for the day I cleaned up. She missed it all.

I am sad we missed out together when my name changed from Madlyn to Deborah.

Sad she missed when I learned to dress myself, to tie my shoes.

My first bike ride, the skinned knees I got from roller-skating down the front steps.

Brushing my hair, then braiding it to keep strands out of my eyes.

The day in sixth grade when I had to squint to see the blackboard, then learned I needed glasses.

The first time I got my period.

My first date.

My high school graduation.

Missed when I learned to stand up straight, shoulders back, so people think I'm confident even when I'm not.

Missed the chance to see my profile like hers.

I'm sad she couldn't show me how to make the cowlicks in my hair, also hers, act right.

How to salve my dry ashy skin.

How to tame the restless tiger inside.

How to cool the blaze in my chest from so many years of masked pain.

She missed my telling of this story.

Then I remind myself—"if only" doesn't go anywhere.
She just didn't.
Some people shoot heroin, others overdose on shame, guilt, and secrets. I'd lost myself in all of it. Drugs were never social entertainment for me; alcohol never just a beverage. They served as my an-

esthesia, a patch, medicine, healing, freedom. And then, near-death. Drugs ruined my every relationship, every corner of my life, because my one true love ruled—alcohol and drugs. I'd hoped this voyage to my homeland would be a tonic in my healing and forgiveness.

Right before I leave the prison's administration building, the warden's assistant waves me into her office. She hands me an inmate bulletin typed on coarse beige newsprint, one page tabbed with a two-inch cutout sketch of a baby.

"Open it," the warden says, her eyes warm, almost teary.

I read,

Further down the hall we're met with gales of laughter and we fought our way in to greet the bubbling, bounding debutante of the compound. The little dark-eyed witch Stromboli, 5 months old, weighing 13 lbs. She is already sporting argyle socks. Her given name is Madlyn Mary but no one seems to remember it. Even Margo, a personality kid herself, has a hard time recalling it. We left laughing, who could help it, behind the force of such a dynamic duo.

MY NAME! MADLYN MARY. There, in black and white, evidence of us together. Even though I learned my name earlier, now it feels real. I run the words over my tongue and imagine our time together in prison, my mom and I, her whispers—Madlyn. My whole body floods with a warm gush of assurance.

It's the end of my tour and the warden walks me to the front of the compound where her house sits near a white picket fence around a four-foot-square grassy area. Inside the fence, six tiny grave markers topple sideways. Bits of moss creep up the white granite.

Her voice softens, almost to a whisper. "These babies didn't make it. You were one of the lucky ones."

I reel inside, ready to break. *How did I end up as one who survived?*

I feel a glimmer of a miracle, how I'd survived against so many odds, beginning on day one of my life. But I don't have time to linger in reflection for long. It's time for my tour to end and the warden leads me farther down the hill. I thank her, we shake hands, and I walk through the prison gates.

Before I drive off in my rental car, I stand in the parking lot and turn to face my first secret—my prison birthplace. The humid air tastes sweet, almost like someone baked bread far off across the Appalachia hills. I feel raw and powerful, as if I can take on anything now, strong right into my muscles like I could lift the asphalt full of cars. For the first time, feeling this exposed gives me hope instead of panic and terror. I've waited my entire life for this—the return, the hope, the dream of my prison.

I drive away, the prison at my back. I've faced my biggest stigma but still don't want to share it with the world. I haven't told my family about my visit to the prison, and informed just a handful of friends.

All this changes three months later when a radio producer calls and leaves me a voice mail.

CHAPTER 15

THE BABY BOOK

WORD ABOUT ME, ABOUT "THE WOMAN born in prison," had spread among wardens, and one tells a reporter about me. She wants a story. But I'd just started to sort it out for myself.

"Deborah, we'd like to interview you inside your birthplace, in your birth mom's prison," a producer from a public radio station says in her voice mail.

It's my prison too.

When I don't call her back, her message the next week tugs my heart.

"We'll air the show on Mother's Day."

"I . . . need time," I say when I call back. "I'll think about it."

MY FIRST RETURN to my prison leaves me with so many treasures, like a vase of clear water, sweet with a most precious bouquet inside. I need to take in its scents, take time to lift each flower, examine it up close and pull its petals apart. I need to absorb the potency of my return, integrate what I'd stashed in the recesses of my brain for two decades. I'd rediscovered the beginnings of my life inch by inch and renewed the bond to my time with my prison mom. But the sweep of stigma about my prison birthplace feels like terrain covered with cactus. I need to deal with it if I want to cast it off.

I need time.

I still don't feel whole. After a lifetime of curiosity, of "I need to discover more," I need even more, not only information but just more. One place to turn—the Feds. Go to the source. Nothing stops me when I'm on a mission.

After my visit to the prison, I petition the Federal Bureau of Prisons in Washington, DC, for my prison mom's file. The privacy officer in DC calls to follow up: "This'll take some time. My job is to read each page and block out any identifying names."

"How long?" I ask and give him a brief one-liner about the urgency. I've waited forever to know about my prison story.

"First," he says, "I must finish another request. I'm in the middle of a privacy review for Al Capone's file. Could take me a month, maybe longer."

Al Capone! I'm right after one serious gangster. Something felt appropriate in this.

One month after I mail my notarized request, a six-pound package of nine hundred pages from the Department of Justice arrives via overnight delivery. Every typed page is marked up with thick black-felt-pen strikeouts to block names and dates. These pages reveal what I never imagined. Before the Bureau removed me from prison, I'd lived with my birth mother for almost a year. A year! Her cell, my nursery. Her bed, did it serve as my crib?

Everything I absorb from her files begins to fill in the blank slate about the woman I'll never hear tell her own story. I glimpse into her soul through typewritten forms, through the eyes of prison officials and caseworkers and piles of letters she wrote about my custody. All her files, they waited for me because she couldn't.

"We never keep these detailed files," my contact at the Bureau says. "I've no idea how these stayed in storage."

Well, I know why. They're meant to fill the void I've carried, to fill the boulder-sized hole in my heart. Good or bad, I'm ready to hear it all. Hit me with the worst of it, because I've already staggered over the coals.

Addiction Data: Drug dependence. Morphine, heroin, cocaine.
Reason for beginning: she states for curiosity sake. She uses heroin
and morphine daily, five shots per day. Needle scars on left wrist. The
patient states she's been vomiting. Court recommends consideration
for parole when cured however she has no insight into her use of
drugs and very little desire to remain off of them.

I'm dying inside. Tears drip onto the paper. *She's in withdrawal*
and who's taking care of her? I wipe the page with my shirtsleeve.
Don't want to spoil my treasured documents. She's locked up—does
anyone notice she needs help? Or does someone just clean up her
puke and leave her to retch again, over and over until the demon
crawls out of her?

Needle scars on left wrist . . . same place as my tattoo, the five-
pointed star inked into me at some beachside dive in San Diego
after I left home.

Sixth of seven children, her father a carpenter of good repute,
made adequate living and parents interested in children but weak in
discipline. Attended various public schools. Completed 10th grade. A
problem from second grade on, taunting, lying, bluffing, defiant.

Hmm, defiant. Maybe I learned this from her. And from the second
grade. Wow, earlier than when I started.

Reported to Juvenile Court by school and police dept. Sent to reform
school for a year, paroled one year later. Worked for Boeing Aircraft
for two months, then given business training, completed her course,
worked for one month until arrested on suspicion of relapse to drugs.
Multiple arrests for drunk [*sic*] and fighting in the street. Given a
probation sentence and released, relapsed at once to the use of drugs.

Oh, I know this one, tough to quit.

Incident after incident, each description excites the rebel in me. But . . . she's a mother, *my* mother. Am I in earnest proud of her or just afraid to make any judgment?

> She was assigned to the prison laundry, an average worker, seemed interested in her work, and had a good attendance record. She stated how working in the laundry she became nervous, upset, and it seemed to her she was going to break down. She shirks work. She has canceled Typing class because of nerves. In all her classes she is respectful and cooperative, but impulsive.

Impulsive—my middle name. I've battled this my whole life and here it is in black and white. Did it come from her?

> Of high average intelligence however it is felt the diagnosis of emotional unstable personality can be made. She has been addicted to narcotic drugs since the age of eighteen years and the prognosis for permanent drug abstinence is considered to be hopeless.

Hopeless? Who says this about a person? About my Margo mother? No one is ever hopeless. *The nerve.*

Then, a series of other incidents:

> Officer called to her several times but she paid no attention and became quite angry and threatened to do something drastic if the officer embarrassed her before the girls again. Contraband razor blades and one penny found in room. At dinnertime she left the mess hall and slammed the door behind her because she was not satisfied with the peas and spread served in place of the potatoes, which were not done. Taken to seclusion.

Multiple times, her reports say, "Good time withheld for month of _____," or, "Taken to seclusion." Over and over the phrases appear: "Reasons checked below: Failure to follow directions." "Lack of concentration." "Warned time and time again."

I can't stand it. She's in the Hole. I start to calculate her total time in solitary confinement but quit, the idea so unbearable. Every month for a week or two at a time, she's in isolation. She's stubborn. Maybe I like the stubborn part, I don't know. I'm a mess of confusion about it all, lost in this fairy tale.

Fight! I want to yell at her, and at the same time, *Get it together, woman!*

I turn to a new section in this foot-high pile of documents. I pump my lungs full of air, as if I've been trapped for hours without oxygen in a coal mine, and read further.

> Since the admission of this inmate, her adjustment has been stormy. She has a long sentence to serve and faced with the prospects of giving birth.

My throat clogs, my heart chokes me, way up out of my chest into my neck and mouth. I can't breathe. Here it is, my story, the beginning of the voyage into sorrow. The saga of Madlyn to Deborah begins.

> She recently attempted to smuggle a letter out of the hospital which she had written to ███████ urging her to write the institution, telling us, "You will come here and take the baby. Tell them you will whether you will or not."

She's still on the scam, trying to work the system, and now it's about me. What mother wouldn't, though?

> At no time has she been above board regarding her plans for the future of the child she was carrying at the time she was received at this institution. At times she indicates she wanted the expected child to be

immediately placed for adoption, however, each time when approached
regarding the matter for a definite plan she would then become
emotional and state she hoped to make plans for some member of the
family to take the child and keep it for her until her release.

I continue to read and turn each page as if I'm pulled into the
middle of a good book I don't want to end, in the middle of a fable,
a myth, not real, none of it. *The Legend of the Baby Born in Prison and
the Inmate Mother Who Would Not Let Go.*

However, she was outspoken in her statement she would not release
the child for adoption but just for a foster home placement. In the
meantime, she has changed her mind and did not want the child to
leave the institution.

"The child." "The baby." *Use my damn name. Just because she's an
inmate with a number doesn't mean we don't have names.*
And "Did not want the child to leave"? *Then what was in her
mind? Did she want us to serve her sentence together?*

When Martha was advised of the plans and the arrangements made,
she became upset, disturbed, emotional, and did everything she knew
to delay the removal of the child from the institution.

I knew it. She loved me and hung on for dear life, our dear lives.

She refused to sign the temporary custody forms and became
belligerent when told this would not delay the child's removal from
the institution.

That's it, fight for me, mama.

She was also of the opinion if she signed the papers, her baby would
be taken from her by the Courts. She wrote the Director of the

Bureau of Prisons a letter and told him she was not letting the baby
leave the institution and requested that plans for the removal of the
baby be postponed.

Straight to the top, right to Washington, DC, to make her plea.
Go for it, Martha Prison Mama.

But she loses her case. Loses me. And I lose her, everything I
needed, all I ever needed. Lost.

And then this:

> She talks a lot about her baby and her plans for the child if she
> can again obtain custody of her when she is released. She has been
> allowed the company of the other girls because of her baby being
> removed from the institution.
>
> She has no insight, is unstable, and is selfish. She has done a lot
> of thinking, whether all of it has been constructive thinking or not.
> At times she still indicates she is interested in the child's welfare,
> she does not want to lose custody of the child and is strong in her
> statement that she plans to make a home for the child upon release.
> She was sincerely fond of her child and has given much thought to it.

My body doesn't have enough space inside for the grief. I'm
about to blow up, smithereens of me blasted out the sliding-glass
door of my third-floor apartment onto the rush-hour street below.
One long, deep wail courses out of me, no tears, just this animal
sound I've never heard before.

I turn to the next page in my baby book, these treasured details
about my start in life. No pink-bowed baby journal with fluffy cloud
stickers to decorate the front cover, these Bureau of Prisons documents record my infant life like no baby book I've ever seen.

> The Welfare Department stated they had continued to work closely
> with Madlyn and pleased to state she was doing well. Madlyn is
> developing into a beautiful child who is adjusting marvelously in the

foster home in which she is placed. In a recent psychological report, Madlyn showed she is indeed a child with high average development at this time. The psychologist added that her unusual spontaneity and vitality react to a wide range of situations and suggests she may be brighter than the present test score. She has, therefore, been highly recommended for adoptive placement.

Every neuron crackles under my skin. I'm outside my body. *Noooo, don't lock down inside, not now.*

They realize this would be a painful procedure for Martha but at the same time stated they must think primarily of the future of this child. Martha has been indifferent to any work other than to care for her baby. She is our worst housekeeper, has accumulated so many things—baby clothes included—that the room is an untidy mess most of the time.

She has settled down materially and appears to be growing up and gaining insight. Of course, in matters pertaining to Madlyn, it is hard to have a true perspective while confined in prison. Matters of this kind cannot be judged fairly when you are not free to do and say as you would in a normal free environment. Martha has a feeling of guilt over having given birth to Madlyn in prison.

They understand, they understand.

I rise to my feet, leave the spread of files and papers fanned across the carpeted floor and lean a shoulder into my sliding-glass patio door. I press my forehead against the cool pane, inhale a world of air. How much more of this can I take? But I can't stop.

CHAPTER SIXTEEN

ANOTHER LETTER

Martha feels now she has grown up to the point if she were free, she could and would accept her responsibilities as a mother and make a home for Madlyn and her son. She seems to be attached to her daughter and we do not want to take the responsibility of placing the daughter elsewhere.

As far as we can ascertain, Martha has never harmed anyone but herself. At an early age she became addicted to narcotics. It might be if given a chance to prove she is sincere at this time, given help and the knowledge if she made good she could keep custody of Madlyn again, it would be the one incentive she needed to straighten up. It is thought she allows her emotions to sway her decisions and she has strong likes and dislikes. However, she can do sound thinking when her emotions are under control.

Under control? You're kidding. Who controls her emotions when they're pregnant and locked up, then delivers in prison and faced with the prospect of losing the baby?

However, she does control herself and tries to prove it when she pleads the court:

I am writing you regarding my baby who was born here. I'd appreciate if you would advise me of my rights concerning this baby. I do not want to lose my baby completely. I want to be able to get her upon my release. Could custody of her be taken from me by the fact

I am in a Government Penal Institution at the present, or because of my past?

I am eligible for a hearing with the Parole Board next year, but I feel as though I don't stand a chance because I already have a different outlook on life since this baby was born.

She fights and fights for me in one last letter.

To County Welfare Department.
When the baby is made ward of the court, does this mean I lose complete custody of her? When I am released can I visit Madlyn? Also, will Mady be moved from home to home? Above all, I do not want Madlyn placed in an institution.

Wait. I'd just left an institution—prison. But she knows this was home for me.
Her letter goes on.

Do the people who have Madlyn want her for other reasons besides an increase of their income? I am going to continue sending money for her care to the best of my ability. My intentions are to regain custody of her upon my release.

I realise your focus is on the child. But please try to understand this experience I am going through is difficult and if I do sound selfish where she is concerned, please know I really have her welfare at heart.

I do not want her to live the life I have. I want her to have love, security and affection.

My heart rips into jagged shards. It's all I'd wanted from her.

And truthfully no matter how much my heart aches, I want to do the best for her. But I also want to know in detail the exact procedure you have to go through to place her.

Since court action has to be taken and if I lose custody, what happens to her if adoption papers are not signed by me? Above all please answer that question. You see, I want Madlyn more than anything in this world, and my love for her is deeply rooted.

If the court isn't in favor of letting me have Madlyn, I wouldn't be so selfish that I would hold ties to cause her any unhappiness in the future.

Please answer my questions as soon as possible, as I need to come to a decision for her welfare in order to have some peace of mind myself.

Sincerely,
Martha

Unbearable sorrow floods me but I need to keep reading. To this day I can't read this letter, though, without falling apart.

COPIES OF THE CORRESPONDENCE I sent in high school to request details of my beginnings lay buried at the end of these files—the same letter mailed several years in a row.

Dear Warden:

I'm writing to get information about my birth and racial origin. All I know is I was born in Alderson, West Virginia in the United States Government Federal Prison for Women. I somehow got separated from my natural mother and placed in an orphanage. I don't know her name. She came from Seattle, Washington, but I have no other information about her, other than she gave birth to a girl.

I am interested in any information you may offer me about my mother, such as nationality of her or my father, her age, present location, and reason for incarceration. It is unlikely that you will reveal my mother's identity, but may I please know her racial origin? May I also have any other information you can disclose about my birth and first history?

I'm sure you can appreciate my desire to learn as much about myself as any ordinary citizen knows. Thank you for considering my request and for any information you might be able to provide me.

All I ever got in return was a cautious letter that the information couldn't be released.

> Dear ████,
> We've heard again from the daughter of Inmate # ████. What shall I tell her this time?
> Sincerely, Warden ████

Page after page, my prison mom pleads in her letters to judges and lawyers and social workers, from coast to coast, begging to keep me. From a prison official:

> To date she has refused to sign the request papers, partly because we think she believes if she does not sign the papers she will delay the child's release from the institution, and because she is of the opinion if she signs the papers her baby will be taken from her by the courts.

My prison mom loses her custody battle, and my story takes the road in these pages.

I'm relieved to read that, by the end of her prison sentence, she found some peace.

> She is a popular member of the inmate group and is the inmate council representative. She is willing and cooperative, willing to do any assignment given her. She volunteers for extra work and does her work well. She attends the movies and other recreation; attends religious services occasionally. She likes and needs approval. Martha is well adjusted to institution routine, but at times is extremely bitter about institutional life and her part in it.

She is kind and understanding of other girls' problems. She is especially thoughtful of those who are ill or handicapped.

I wonder, Did my compassion come from her?

IT FEELS WRONG but I'm proud like a parent impressed with her child's school report. But it's my mother's prison record, for crying out loud. I still can't quite grasp this truth, this discovery, the whole thing.

Then, there it is, in one of the last letters about my placement. A hint but not a definitive answer about my race, still the unknown.

> From the very first, although Martha would one minute say she wanted the baby placed for adoption, she would later state she wanted to make other arrangements. She received a letter from ▆▆▆▆ stating if the baby had no Negro blood in her, she [the letter writer] would try to place it with some reliable family. If possible, Martha wants her child adopted by someone who would permit her to visit the child.

Whoa. Someone said this? Damn.

My mom apparently refused to respond to this letter, because it was sent several times to her. Thus, she's left me with a lifetime of unknowns. I can either battle or embrace this mystery of "one drop," which, according to archaic law, defines someone as Black or biracial.

WHAT FOLLOWS WARMS my heart—a list of my first formula, prison-style:

> The baby medical reports are as follows—fed every three hours during the day and once during the night on the following formula:
>> One, thirteen (13) ounce liquid can of Carnation milk
>> One equal can of water
>> Seven tablespoonsful of White Karo syrup.

Boil H2O, mix syrup, then pour into container with milk. Mix and place bottle. Martha states she usually places at least seven ounces in bottle but the baby does not always take this amount at each feeding. The baby is also given baby food such as strained vegetables and meats twice a day, at 2:00 o'clock and 6:00 o'clock. She drinks whole milk and orange juice.

This tenderness sweeps through me about the feeding schedules and strained foods in prison.

The documents also expose pieces of the story about my foster care and, for the first time, I learn that my placement into adoption was finalized at around age three or four. The courts had granted my parents custody when I was two or three, but the courts didn't release me legally until Margo signed relinquishment papers. She took her own sweet time, several years, to do this.

SOME OF MY toddler time falls into place at last. I can't tell how many foster homes I was placed in, and as an adult, I don't remember any of it. My destiny took many unexpected turns. I went from West Virginia to Seattle, then, a few years later, to Rome for my father's sabbatical year, from a world of color to one without, from stories of the street to the Louvre, Fellini films, and *Marat-Sade* on stage. One of the documents discusses possible foster placement in West Virginia. So many "possibles" haunt me. What if the authorities had placed me in foster care in the Appalachian Mountains instead of Seattle? Might I be a coal miner's daughter instead of the daughter of two English professors? Rather than going to temple with my parents, I could've spent Sundays in Alderson's Baptist church.

I flip through the files and root for her—"Right on" for my rebel prison mother. Prison didn't even kill her spirit. Something comforts me as I read these documents. Some of them answer how close my apple is to her tree. I understand her fervor and fight, her fierce, illogical stubbornness, her impassioned view of the world. It all lives in me, too.

I understand more her conflicts and struggles, but why couldn't she stay clean? Why was each release just a pause in her prison career? Because she faced complex and impossible choices.

Then it strikes me: She didn't leave me. I left her. I left her locked up when I was scooped out of her cell in the middle of the night and taken into the free world. I left her behind—how can I feel anger towards her?

How can I feel anything but infinite anguish about our severed bond?

In the end she fought hard for custody but the courts decided: "Prison is no place to raise a child." Torn from the one love of my first twelve months, *the* most important developmental stage in a child's life, I was unmoored and set to sail.

Maybe the rage I cast against my adoptive mother—the broken hand, the murder plot, the fire setting—maybe all this was meant for my prison mother. But I don't think so. Maybe I should be angry about her part in the whole drama of my life, angry about her addiction, her crimes, her lifestyle, her multiple prison sentences, her lack of mental and emotional wellness, her shooting up while pregnant with me. Am I in denial about my anger towards her? I can't find it.

IN THE MIDDLE of the prison files I land on a letter from one of my foster mothers to my prison mom and in this one flip of a page, every single bit of self-image I'd held about my younger self is redefined.

Monday night 10:15

Dear Martha,

I hope you will forgive me for calling you by your first name, but in a way I think your darling little daughter is introduction enough.

I've had Mady ever since she was brought out here so have learned to love her very much. Until now I didn't feel I could write you, but was given permission by my new worker for Madlyn. He has been the worker for the 2 other babies here so I was glad to have him take over for Mady too. He is such a wonderful person I know you will like him too.

I know the only thing you are particularly interested in is this little daughter of yours so I am going to try to tell you all the things I would want to know if I hadn't seen my baby for so long.

First of all she is in excellent health and cute as a button. She weighed 19 pounds 2 ounces and is 28 inches tall. She has been walking ever since the week before her birthday, but if she is in a big hurry she will sometimes crawl even yet. I haven't tried to do much toilet training for she is still rather young, however, if she is wearing training panties and puddles it breaks her heart. But if she has a diaper and plastic panties on she doesn't see what she has done and it means nothing to her. She has just started coming and telling me after she has messed her panties, and of course that is the first step, then later she will tell me before it happens.

I have 3 children of my own, a girl 10 and 2 boys who are 12 and 15, and have kept many foster children in my home but can honestly say we have never had one quite as sweet or smart as your little Madlyn.

My husband actually makes a fuss over her more and takes her with him more than he ever did any of his own when they were little. We have all really fallen in love with her, and I am glad to say she is a happy little girl here.

I knew it, sensed it—I was happy before my adoption. Prison as my birthplace wasn't the problem. Neither was my foster care. Multiple moves from family to family took their toll on me. The letter goes on:

She has taken her milk only from a glass ever since coming to us, and is the best little eater we ever had. She says many words now, and understands practically everything said to her even though she tries to ignore some things.

The first words she learned were *Hi kid!* to my oldest boy every morning when she was brought out of her crib. She also says bye bye, no no, doggy, keekee (for kitty), Bobby, Bibby (for Billy), all gone, horsey, cookie, candy, I ub oo (for I love you), gink (for drink), ta too (for thank you), Daddy, Mommy, sissy, baby, tickle tickle, and her toes are Piggy Piggy. She also says bad boy and bad baby, nie nie for nighty night, and how do.

She loves to play peek but is a little tease and instead of covering her face with her hands she puts them to one side and peeps around them.

She is a friendly baby and makes up with strangers quickly. Everyone who has known her loves her.

I took the pictures of her on her Birthday for I knew you would want to have them. The new little baby they just brought to me I am taking pictures of every week so the parents who adopt her will have a record of her tiny baby days too. I have several other snapshots of Mady I will also save for you. We had enlargements made of three of these Birthday ones and they are just beautiful. If you would like to borrow the negatives to have some made when you get back I would be glad to lend them to you.

I am sorry I cannot tell you our names or where Mady is, but when it is time the Welfare Department will give you the information. In the meantime I will try to write and send pictures now and then so you can see how beautiful your baby is growing.

Now to tell you some of the cute little things she does. I think the cutest is the way she loves to fight and argue with her Daddy. She has learned to go up and downstairs very well now, but at first we were afraid she would take some bad tumbles so we tried to keep her down.

Whenever we saw her start up we stood at the bottom and scolded and shook our finger at her. Of course she just laughed for she is such a tease, but it got so she would start up just for the argument, and if we didn't argue she'd come back down and start up again. Ours is a wrought iron stairway that runs up behind our large fireplace, and she goes up a few steps and sticks her arms out through the iron bars and shakes her fist and hollers and scolds until her Daddy goes over and does the same. She talks and jabbers more than any youngster we ever saw. I think every word of it means something to her, and sometimes I'm glad I don't know what she is saying. Ha!

Chatty? Friendly and jabbers? My tiny-baby days. This is me before the mute, insecure, scared little girl who suffocated in melancholy.

My foster mother reveals more than I ever imagined I'd learn about my early years:

When she looks through magazines she has started wetting her fingers to turn the pages for she has seen us do it.

We always know when she is ready for a nap for she sucks her thumb and tweaks one ear or a lock of hair. One day she fussed to go to bed and I was busy with the tiny new baby so she went on upstairs. After I finished changing the baby I followed her up, she was standing with her head leaning against my daughter's bed, her thumb in her mouth, and she was practically asleep. She couldn't get over the side and into her own bed so she did the next best.

When we feed her she always says "all gone" when her plate is empty, but if it isn't empty and she doesn't want any more she still says "all gone." After the "all gone" we know she is full.

My husband drives a school bus and has a car seat fixed on one of the seats just behind his driver's seat so she can go along on the bus rounds. If the bus leaves without her there really is war in the house for a while until she forgets, and then, when he gets back home and she watches him back it into the driveway she starts scolding all over again.

She loves the new baby even though she is still a little jealous. She likes to watch me change her and I let her rub the powder on her tummy and bring me diapers. If I say "nice baby" she draws out a big long Ohhhhhhhh and then leans over and kisses her, but if she has something in her hand she is just as liable to hit her one after the kiss. She isn't selfish for she puts all kinds of toys in bed with the baby and wonders why she doesn't play with them.

I don't think I told you she has 5 teeth and will have the 6th before long. Teething is the only thing she's been slow in, but she made up for it in so many other ways.

Well, I just can't think of anything more right now, but if there are some other things you would like to know you might write my worker and he can let me know. I do hope you like the pictures, and I wish I were able to send the enlargements so you could really see how darling she is.

Please don't ever fear she isn't receiving good care. We love her like one of our own and wouldn't let anything happen to her for the world.

Sincerely,
Mady's foster mother

P.S. Look at the pictures in the order they were taken and they are more interesting. I have them numbered on the front.

I lean back in the chair and sit in all the bigness of how love surrounded me in my early years. Tears seep from my eyes into the paper but I don't want to ruin the page so I press a folded, dry washcloth across the bridge of my nose to catch the drips.

FOR SOME REASON, I never once blame my prison mother for her fight to keep me in prison. She wanted her baby girl. But what if she'd lost custody of me at birth? Or if she'd relinquished me of her own free will right away? Would I have felt less restless and on edge with an earlier separation, more secure, suffered less?

The documents help me understand that I can't outrun my birth mother or the traumas of my first years. I guess a girl can love just so many mothers. I must've closed the door on Mother with too many before her.

On the next page, one of the last, a document reinforces the agony and brings to life the end of our short story together.

She is a deep imprint stitched to my back.

CHAPTER SEVENTEEN

THE TELEGRAM

Telegram—Gov't. Rate

To: United States Marshal, Federal Building, Seattle, Washington

Baby Girl Doe, escorted by Federal Agent ███ will arrive Northern Airways, Wednesday 4:55 A.M. with Inmate # ████'s Baby Girl Doe. Please reserve hotel room and leave message at Airport where she is to go.

Warden ████

Inmate #'s Baby Girl Doe? I'm unnamed? In one swipe I lose my mother-source and my name. Why would they use this placeholder name, in most cases meant to protect the identity of a crime victim or a witness? I'm neither. Or maybe I am a witness. I did, after all, behold what few others have seen, even though I don't remember it. Who knows what I witnessed? I can only imagine.

This telegram, more than anything else, sends me deeper into panic and sadness about the night I left her behind, the separation almost like a big, enforced escape at the crack of dawn. The telegram also helps one more piece fall into place about the mystery. Now it's clear why I've vomited on airplanes, why the trapped diesel smell brings on nausea. It's an association from infancy, a conditioned response, even though I love to travel and fly. Infants and toddlers gauge their environments by what adults convey, and I traveled with a stranger, the federal marshal, about to enter a void, the wide unknown, even worse than the void of the Hole.

CHAPTER EIGHTEEN

YARN TOY—MORE EVIDENCE

THE LAST FORM, THE LAST PAGE in my baby book, closes one of the many open circles in my life, evidence of my prison mother's continued love, in her handwriting.

Authorization To Mail Package Out Of Institution

Inmate No. ████████

is authorized to ship from the institution the following items to the address below c/o the County Welfare Department:

1 yarn dog

My treasure, my beloved yarn toy, its journey to me with this prison authorization, like a ticket for precious cargo about to set sail on an ocean liner.

Six other separate requests follow, more proof of her continued love for me:

1 crocheted baby dress
1 crocheted baby bib
1 pair of crocheted infant slippers
3 sweaters (child's)
1 stuffed doll
1 knit cap

I wish I could see them. *Where are they? What happened to them?*

The yarn toy, though, has followed me since the beginning, final evidence of our severed love. Her hands wound and wove every strand, the last indirect touch I have from my prison mother.

CHAPTER NINETEEN

LESS AFRAID OF
THE DARK CORNERS

SOMETHING PULLS ME TO RETURN, and this time it's not out of curiosity about my prison mom or desperation about my roots. This time it's because I'm grateful for my freedom, my transformation. I'm also conscious that it could've been me who was locked up for the rest of my life. After all the hurt I've inflicted on others, I'm called to give back, to reach out where I'm comfortable and welcomed with open wide arms: women's prisons.

It's as if I'm on autopilot on a path I was born to stomp along. As if born with a job.

Untreated mental health issues can take a person down along with others around her. I lived it. Mental health support averted my future violence and curbed my addictions. In my previous life I tick-ticked inside, a time bomb ready to blast anyone in my path with the shrapnel of my anger. I hate to admit that if I'd refused to confront my disturbed self, I would've been a prime candidate for committing the kind of tragedy we read in the front-page news. The churn of fury so vast inside me all those years, it needed its own zip code, a rage in multiples of pi. I stood always on a precipice of you-never-know-when irrational violence, and it's a miracle I didn't just snap one day. A miracle I didn't plot more and let loose on total strangers, or more against my mother and father and brother, or my teachers, or neighbors. Even worse, I'm not sure I would have felt remorse then.

I RETURN TO prisons, my birthplace, and address the inmates there. My story is a natural fit for the women, and I share what I've learned, how life is less about what happens and more about what we do with what happens. Not a new idea, just one that takes practice to believe and to live day by day. I use my life to show how we're all more than the sum of our parts.

Aren't we all more than the worst things we've ever done? It's possible to fulfill this any time we choose to walk out of our history and begin new, whenever we want to transcend and triumph. I'm proof of this. Of course, we can't do it alone, but if we search, we'll find others willing to help. One of the best influences we can have on our communities and the world at large is to grow in self-awareness.

As I speak in prisons, almost every head in the audience nods, incarcerated and staff alike. The women smile, show me I'm meant to follow this vision. On occasion I'll conduct a writing workshop with women in prisons, and in one of my first, in a high-security unit, an officer leads me into a double-paned, glass-enclosed classroom with a guard stationed outside. Twenty women lean over their blank papers at two long folding tables, the same tables they use in the mess hall. Everyone calls them "girls," no matter if they're seventeen or seventy. They call me Teacher.

We open with an informal talk session. We chat and laugh, and some cry. Then they begin to set their thoughts down on paper, and most times no one knows what to write. The women shuffle their pages as I fire out story-starter ideas.

On the second workshop day, they write about their parents. One inmate blurts out in the middle of the workshop, "When I was six I tried to run away from home because a neighbor, a friend of the family, forced me to eat human waste and no one did anything."

I ache for her.

The women feel safe telling their stories in this circle. A corner of their filters drops—they know I won't judge.

The woman goes on. "Then my mother pointed her pistol and shot at me. She pulled the trigger, and I didn't know if the gun was empty or not."

My life hasn't been so bad after all, I think.

Another woman looks straight ahead, listening. She's the self-proclaimed in-house prison preacher and always quotes Bible verses to get everyone else into her religious groove. She's also the queen of plucked eyebrows, arched to give herself a surprised look. A clunky cross hangs on her neck. "Sounds like a crazy woman," she says about the inmate's mother.

The woman goes on and on. "My mother whipped me with coat hangers, extension cords, or twigs off trees. Did I already mention the crow bar? But she didn't ever shoot when she held a gun on me."

I'm taking this all in, letting the stories roll.

Another woman, sprawled in her chair, interrupts the woman's story about her mother. "You think God's watching over? I'd say your spiritual bubble is gonna bust."

Just then a woman turns to me and says, "Hey! You're talking to a bunch of women with low self-esteem."

I said I know, but I haven't been the one talking. They have.

Once the group settles down, I say, "Now write a list of things that make you mad. Not only what's pissed you off in here but also in your own lives."

That's all it takes. Everyone dives in. No one's ever asked them before to detail what makes them mad. They all scribble page after page and rack up lists of unjust events.

Then I suggest they pick one event from their list and write a story about it. It gets wild then! Topics like war, hunger, injustice. It gets big. They go around the tables and start to read their stories. They cheer and hoot—until the preacher woman's turn.

Her list turns out to be what's important to her: "God, guitars, women, and cowboy boots."

"I just got outta thirty-day lockup," she adds, "for stealing someone's cigarettes and then lying and picking a fight about it."

She says she's also angry I'd had to cancel two earlier workshops. I tell her she would've missed out anyway because of her lockup time in segregation.

The women fall silent. No one has ever talked back to the preacher woman.

It turns out she had more lockup time than I had with my scheduled workshops. She never shows up again in one of my workshops.

THESE PRISON WORKSHOPS show how redemption is made possible by hope. Hope alone won't solve anything. Yet without hope, nothing's possible.

I take myself into a bigger dream, visiting prisons in New York, California, Connecticut, on both coasts, North and South. I zigzag around the country, and women line up to fill metal folding chairs in prison gyms, and we shake hands, hug if allowed, and dig deep into our souls. Their openness moves me like nothing else I've ever known.

Back home, Mother's condition has stabilized but she's still in and out of chemo treatments. I feel guilty I'm enmeshed in the depths of everything prison and prison mom. She'd take it as betrayal, yet I couldn't love her more or mourn losing her more. The timing, though . . . I have no control. I haven't told her or anyone in my family what I'm up to.

I TRAVELED FROM prison to prison, across the country, to lead basic writing-skills and creativity workshops with incarcerated women, thrilled to witness hidden talents emerge. It took me this long before I was comfortable in front of people. At last I stepped out of my solitude.

Four months into my prison tours, I received an envelope from the Federal Bureau of Prisons. I opened it and pulled out one of their internal newsletters. Right on the front page, there I was. I stared, horrified. No one had asked my permission. I became their poster girl for the "bad girl gone good."

The article revealed my rough beginnings and credited my return as a speaker and writer working with female inmates as the first program of its kind in the federal prison system. I clutched the paper, semiproud of my origin. I didn't think I'd ever boast about it. However, I was no longer ashamed of my birthplace. It was just a location—unique, but still just a place and still loaded with the emotions of my story.

Yet, it's a place I was private about. Not secretive, but protective about judgment from others. Every piece that touched my life had the potential to stir prejudice and heated opinions: prison, inmates, the Appalachia Mountains, the South, Jews, adoption, foster care, race, addiction. All these threads in the web of my story, all ripe for passionate and sometimes negative judgment. I felt safest when I stepped away from judgment.

Most of all I was protective of my mother in prison, her addiction, her street life, her crimes and many sentences, even her victories and accomplishments, as well as the details of our time together. She endured what no mother should ever face. Some mothers decide to relinquish their babies at birth. Some, as much as they later lament the decision, feel like it was their best option at the time.

Mothers in prison struggle with so little access to resources and emotional support, and in general, society looks down on inmates as second class, especially women. I hold the highest respect for my prison mom. She's not here to say, "Tell it, tell it all, baby." This is as much the story of both my mothers—Margo and Mother—as it is mine. It's my pocket of truth, one I don't want tainted by public opinion or publicized into sensationalism.

About this time, other radio interview requests poured in about my prison tours and birthplace, about my birth circumstances, along with inquiries from several literary agents and editors, who encouraged me to weave my life story into a book. I'm not a tell-all kind of person nor was I interested in putting one more motivational book into the marketplace. I loved to read them. I just didn't want to write the one I was asked to write before this one.

Yet I tried. I sat for hours with pen in hand, but words do not fly in on wings. Still, I came up with the one sentence that tipped my world: Secret letter reveals heroin-addicted prison birth. But the rest of my story was jumbled in my brain, and I didn't know how to untangle it.

I withdrew from the dialogues with agents and editors but then several film producers heard about "the woman born in prison." The last thing I wanted was any part of a film about my life, so I retreated even more. Why would I want to relive pain and loss? I wasn't ready to claim my criminal escapades in public nor the fear, rage, and insecurities that punctuated my life's every moment for most of my days.

OVER TIME, WITHOUT pressure from strangers to write my story, a light goes on. I'm less and less afraid of the dark corners, less terrified of my own story with its twists and turns. I've grown to understand how secrets don't destroy us, but the keeping of secrets can kill us. It takes more energy to keep up an act and hold in a secret than it does to face the truth.

Maybe it's time to share the pieces I want, the way I want.

IT'S A FEW weeks into Mother's first chemo treatments. A month before her eightieth birthday, I visit her and can't shake the heartache, can't bear how her sturdy body has withered into a pile of limbs. I plan a surprise birthday party, even though any notice of her, especially an elegant, catered bash, and in her condition, is the last thing she'd want. She's from a generation of women who always want to highlight others. But I hope she'll appreciate it, even in her illness. Dad assures me she's okay.

Mother, now weak and frail, weighs just under a hundred pounds. I feel it's her last birthday, our last together. Some years before she'd said: "When I am eighty, I don't want just a night out to dinner."

But I know my father doesn't have it in him to plan a big celebration, and even if he did, this is my present to make up for the resentment I carried about Mother's past birthdays, and for the birthdays ahead we'll never share.

I need to make up for all those years I hated Mother's birthday parties because I wanted the parties to celebrate a different mother. I must show Mother my enduring love. And I need to plan this all by myself.

My father brings Mother to Minneapolis where I've rented a huge formal dining hall. She inches into the room packed with sixty-plus people: her siblings and nieces and nephews, our New England family, and friends who flew in from around the country. I'd even located her dearest college roommate, who showed up. What an emotional moment, two old women in reunion after a lifetime of separation. They embrace one another like schoolgirls.

Mother and I, along with Jonathan and my father, sit at the head table. Everyone is amazed by the bond Mother and I built after our estrangement, and they're surprised, too, at my effort to host this elaborate event. Sadly, they're also surprised my mother is still alive. She's a bag of bones in her red silk dress, the sash wrapped around her waist to hide her colostomy bag. The toasts fill the air, a spectacular send-off for what comes next.

AFTER A YEAR of chemo, Mother's bedridden, and in-home hospice care covers her around the clock. I can't stand what I learn—hospice means limited time, six months or less.

I continue to fly to Chicago every weekend. I've become less and less nauseated when I fly, but airplane air can still make me a little queasy. Whenever a plane begins its descent and I prepare to land, panic blows up inside me, and I feel as if I'm in trouble, have done something wrong. The only way I've come to understand this is as a body memory—the physical symptom doesn't appear related to any physical cause in the moment. It must relate to my first flight, where I imagine I sensed all the anxiety about my future.

I CREDIT-CARD DEBT my air travel to Mother's bedside, weekend after weekend for many months. I massage her feet, read to her. I hold her bony hand, the hand of the woman who reached for mine while I pulled away, the hand of the woman who stood by me all these years. I nestle at her side and we nap together. On one visit, I lean over her hospital bed, set up in my father's study opposite his teak desk, and brush wisps of her chemo-thinned white hair off her fevered brow, the way she mopped my little girl forehead when I bent over the toilet, nauseous, my forehead hot with sweat.

"Sorry," I whisper in her ear, beside her in bed.

She turns.

It's too much for either of us to name what we're sorry about.

"I love you, Pet," she says.

I swallow. I no longer hate her words of love. I revel in them. We weep together. I cry with guilt over all those years of rejecting her, how I injured her spirit. Her tears, I imagine, are also for all of our past losses.

My mother's rich olive-colored skin is now beige and draped, like wet masking tape stuck on a stick. Her once-muscled forearms rest like twigs on her bedcovers. She's too weak to reach for me, never mind a full embrace. It's been over a month since she's mustered enough strength to meet me at the airport or even dial the phone, so I don't expect her arms to lift and welcome me anymore.

But the eyes, her full brown eyes, still shine, clear with her love for me. They speak their own language even though she's spent from dying and her face cannot manage an expression. Not one glimmer in her eyes speaks of death around the corner, of her apprehension or relief or maybe fear. Maybe not fear.

My hands volunteer themselves. One runs its fingers through her few silver wisps of hair. My other hand caresses her back, finds its own rhythm, and my fingers ripple over most every vertebra and rib while I stroke with repetition from the nape of her neck down to her waist.

My mother's hands used to fret. Her busy fingers knit the air. I understand why from those years of my agitated youth, my extended youth to thirty or so. After we bonded, though, devoted daughter and mother, what made her fingers fret?

I consider my mother's hands, and her socks, dozens of socks I bring for her on visits. Soft tan cotton socks, nothing too tight at the ankle, white sport socks, short argyle wool ones, maroons and more tan and more white and another wool, any color. I buy in excess for her then: underwear, socks, robes, nightgowns. All the socks for her to sit around, lay down in, socks to fit her swollen ankles and feet, bloated from cancer sweeping to her liver, skin stretched at her ankles like fruits ready to burst with ripeness. Her favorite—blue fluffy socks—she wears like slippers, at night in bed, then days in bed.

The next day, before I leave her bedside, Mother and I discuss my unexpected desire for children.

"But I'm single right now," I tell her. My latest relationship has just ended. "And what if with kids I won't find time to follow my creative work?"

"Women have raised children for centuries," she says, "in all kinds of circumstances and all kinds of relationships, single or not."

She smiles and I hug her. She encourages me to do whatever I want. Kids, career, writing, travel, everything together.

All of a sudden I recognize the truth of my mother. She's a courageous pioneer. She's been one all along. In my judgment as a child, I believed she and Dad adopted me to boost their liberal image. I guess those thoughts helped me block them out.

Mother, ten years older than my father, adopted me while in her forties. Even more unusual, she adopted a multiracial girl, as though oblivious to the rarity of our blended family.

My parents, already outsiders themselves as Jews in academia, marched around with their little caramel-colored girl, innovators in a segregated, pre–civil rights America, where races never integrated in private.

I want to be brave for her, give her whatever I can.

"Mother, do you ever wonder about the phone call from the police? Do you . . . want to hear about those years I disappeared?"

She smiles.

"Thanks. Not really."

CHAPTER TWENTY

BLUE SOCKS

IT'S THANKSGIVING. FOR THE FIRST TIME in many years, eight of us gather at my parents' house at the same time: Mother, Dad, my brother, his wife, their three young children, and me.

Jonathan wheels Mother to the family table but she refuses food. I try to tempt her with a spoon of whipped cream to her lips but she turns her face away. Something feels different about Mother. After dinner I call the hospice nurse. While we wait, I massage her feet through the fluff of her blue socks.

"Don't stop. Don't go," she says, her gaze straight into mine. She stares beyond me and into me at the same time. I hold this look, possess it, this horizon together and fight an instinct to avert my eyes.

"Stay with her, stay," I command myself. Every speck of courage in me gathers for this one moment. I refuse to look away. My father on the other side of the room holds her bottle of morphine, his face directed down like he's reading the label, but his eyes peer over his glasses. He watches us, her, his wife of almost fifty years, from twelve feet away.

Within the hour the nurse arrives, races to Mother's bed, then calls us together in the hall outside her room. "She's close to death," the nurse whispers. She turns to me. "Would you like to accompany me alone with her for a minute?"

I stare at her, air trapped in the bottom of my lungs. I panic.

"I'm going to wash her body, help soothe her," she says.

I know she asked me for this daughter-mother aloneness, but I can't. A private and proud woman, Mother would never want me to see her naked on her deathbed. More than this, though, in truth I am scared. Terror engulfs me. *Go*, I tell myself, *do it anyway*, but I can't.

Now I wish I'd been able to wash and help soothe my mother. And at the same time, I think she would've hated it. Or would she?

I wait outside Mother's room in the hall. Then, after a few minutes, the nurse calls my father, brother, and me into her room. I want to beg for mercy. To whom, though? *Please, not now, not again. Please. No. Don't.* My plea, not to Mother, not to anyone in particular. I know she needed to go. I want her free from suffering.

But I want her. I need her. I need not to lose another mother.

I glance at the clock. It's 11:15 p.m., the exact time the prison documents record for my time of birth. On the dot.

I stroke Mother's hair with one hand and wrap my other around her bony shoulder. Dad stands opposite me, my brother next to him. Mother lurches and takes her last breath. The thought flashes through me: Did she wait to die until I arrived? I lean down, my lips close to her ear. "Thank you, Mother. You'll always be with me." I raise my voice. I want to make sure my words reach her. I need her to hear I value her.

I embrace my mother in her final gasp. She shudders in this dying, and fear makes me retreat. I jump. It's her lurch for air, the suddenness. No one told me, not the hospice nurse, not my father or my older brother. I'd never read about this. It is not like this in movies. I never leaned so close to death.

No one warned me about the deep-lung death gurgle, and how my hands would want to reach for her. All I have is touch, then the sound of her dying. Soon the touch and sound end, my hands empty in the silence.

THE MORTUARY DRIVERS take an hour to arrive, and I covet the time alone with Mother. My brother and father had left the room right after she took her last breath.

I kiss her cheeks, her forehead, the way she kissed mine to check my fever. I sit at her side and hold her quiet hands, cry, and stop. Cry and stop.

I stand at the foot of her bed and wrap my fingers around her ankles, around her blue socks. I jiggle her with a slight rock, left right left, then a soft shake to see if any life has lingered. Is it real? Nothing. She's still warm. And dead.

Images of my mother's anguished disintegration cover me, images of her dying moments, the urgent vitality of her life flowing away in her last minutes. A wind sweeps through me, nothing I'd ever felt before in my body, like someone has attached a fireplace bellows to me and puffs and puffs a long constant breeze through my neurons. Not air. Not sky. A breath maybe. Electricity and breath into my every cell.

THEN I OPEN the nightstand beside her bed and discover an empty tissue box with a piece of paper peeking out. I'm snooping like I did when I found the prison letter.

I pull out the note, her last shopping list—*anchovies, capers, the bank*—scribbled on a scrap of paper, along with *bread, the pharmacy*. Pushed into one corner of the drawer in the back sits a clear-plastic rectangular box packed with lined-up bobby pins.

I then wander into the garage, open the glove compartment of my mother's car, and dig around. Lodged under irregularly folded state maps, my fingertips land on a cough-drop tin filled with a collection of quarters, for parking I figure. I pocket and save the tin of coins and box of bobby pins.

Back at her bedside, I open her nightstand drawer again and find, further buried, a banded-together stack of postcards. It's the preaddressed cards we had mailed to each other during my summer camp in England, before everything turned bad.

Dear Mother,

One of the cooks let me help her in the kitchen. We made toast and maenase with oil and egg yoke. Our wether has been fine exsept for at night it rains hard. Don't forget to send me pencils. I miss you. But I am not home sick yet.

One of the horses is lame so today there were only two horses to ride. My first lesson I made the horse trott. I like fast. On the farm there are 3 horses, 2 pigs, two cows and a calf. We play games like baseball. I like sports.

Love and kisses, Debbie

Deb Dear:

Don't worry about the stains on your sweater. It's too bad if the stains don't come out, but things like this do happen when children play. Remember to put all of your clothes together—wear your jacket and mittens, and pack your raincoat. Your father and I both get excited at the thought of seeing you soon. I go back to London tomorrow—Monday.

Remember your manners. Be sure you thank everyone.

Love, Mother

Dear Mother,

I don't think I ever want to go away again. Whenever I am lonesome I worry about you. I am having a JOLLY good time.

Today I went to the sea for the whole day. We ate lunch and drank tea there. It's fun buried up to my neck in the sand. At first when I went in the water I got scared then I got use to it. The waves are JOLLY big.

Love, Debbie

AS THE MORTUARY workers roll Mother's body towards the door on a gurney, I shadow the attendants. I'm thankful she and I said everything we needed to say to one another before she passed away.

They load her into a body bag, all the life, all the fight in her gone. My mind taunts me with my battle against her, with all she endured. How did she wait for me so long? How did she stand by me through all I did to her?

I want—need—to give her more, and she's gone.

Gone. Death does not honor our desperation for a second chance. Nor does it obey the cry for reconciliation.

That night, I pull on all my mother's socks, one over the other, all the socks except the blue ones she died in. She was cremated in her blue socks.

Hopelessness tries to drag me down into its hole but I won't let it. I need to prove to myself and to Mother my love for her, my respect. A stranger to the temple, back in Minneapolis I attend the mourner's service every night and I sit Shiva for 365 consecutive sundowns and recite Kaddish, the Jewish prayer for mourning. I haven't done any one thing in my life for 365 consecutive days. My orthodox uncles who taught me the prayer do it for seven days. But I can't—won't—stop. My devotion to the mourner's service shocks everyone, most of all me.

GRIEF BITES AND stings. I need to occupy and distract myself, and while I might not have the DNA for impulse control, I discover in those first twelve months without Mother my extra gene for quirky, off-the-wall creativity. I sink my sorrow into the only outlet left, since I no longer drink or drug, and put my nonlinear, bouncy brain to good use and invent a few products. The creativity helps lift the shroud of constant sadness. I work nonstop, with a fount of ideas. Some tank, but I don't care because I don't call mistakes failure.

My father begins his descent into the horrific world of mind subtraction: Alzheimer's. My time's up on a new life designed to care for myself and focus on my work.

CHAPTER TWENTY-ONE

RETURN TO THE VEILED LADY

MY FATHER'S DAILY HOUR-LONG WALKS TURN into all-day wanderings into neighborhoods where we can't find him. His repetitions of "Where are we?" and his empty gaze give us clues he needs to see a doctor. My father's disappearance cell by cell reminds me that I adored some things about him, qualities I'd forgotten because of his eruptions of violence.

His capacity for deep compassion and ease with his emotions brought me close to the most tender side of this man. He'd often shed tears when he heard a story about someone in need. And he held great admiration and respect for laborers and blue-collar work—maybe that was the socialist in him.

When I was in high school and still living at home, one night after dinner I broke a teacup in my mother's china collection and felt terrible. My mother lit into me, but my father defended me. "She feels bad enough," he said, "no need to scold her." That was it. I felt released from the guilt and protected by my father.

On one of his last travels alone, I took him to the airport and we sat over tea at a table by a window. He asked me, out of nowhere, "Do I dominate you?"

Right in front of me, I knew then where I learned my blunt honesty.

He must have sensed how my walls of protection and tension built up in his presence.

"Yes," I told him.

That's all we said. But his question caused me to reflect. We had a special way with each other, soft moments clouded by his infrequent and unexpected violence. And then there was our contest of wills, the special way I knew to aggravate him on purpose, to provoke him.

THE DAY MY father finds out he is losing his mind, he can't recall two-syllable words on the doctor's orders. *Table, walnut, diving.* He says he sees them swim away, first one, then the other two. Words float from a once measured vocabulary. After a lifetime of scrutinizing *Paradise Lost*, he replies, "Alas, I thought as much," the day doctors diagnose dementia. It's his dancing companion, this madness, for the next ten years.

"Don't much like the idea of an existence without my mind," he tells me on one of our visits to the neurologist. "Toenails," he adds. "After the mind goes, there is not much left but toenails."

Thank God for toenails, I think. At least there's something left.

The scholar melts into a slow drip through stages of childhood. He reads books with the pages turned upside down. He thumps the wall with the palm of his hand next to the elevator button in the lobby of his assisted-living center, his face puzzled as to why the elevator won't respond to his wall banging. Pained and fascinated at the same time, I witness the curse of my father's Alzheimer's. The disease steals his critical, cerebral style, yet as the intellectual professor fades, Dad softens. It's also the first time in my life I see his face open, without a beard, and his gentleness glows from his cheeks.

AS DIFFICULT AS I found my father and as much as I rejected my mother, they and their friends influenced me in the deepest of ways. They introduced me to great writers, painters, a few physicists, all family friends who dined and drank at parties at our house every month, sometimes twice a month. My parents kept a social household, and their literary circle impacted my worldview about marching to your own drumbeat. Some were gay or lesbian, some drank like pirates, or were depressed or flew between highs and lows on who-knows-what, and some were institutionalized with off-and-on "insanity," as my parents would describe it.

I can't say I learned to write from this exposure, although I'm sure all those nights of poetry readings helped me fall in love with words and the sound of language. Since I never talked, I listened a lot.

I'm also sure my early rebellion against academia and what I viewed then as artistic and literary arrogance stems from this background.

A FEW YEARS before my father dies, my life as a mother begins. Motherhood never seemed possible in my former life. *How can I raise children and care for others when I couldn't even take care of myself?*

My father and I become a little closer before he passes away because I like him better with his tender side, even if it's in dementia. I'm also shocked how his regression parallels the same stages of development as my now seven-year-old daughter—only in reverse.

The night he dies, my daughters and I visit him. My youngest, then around three, holds his hand and tucks her little yarn-toy lamb on his pillow, right by his ear. He is on his way out, nonresponsive other than the moment when his body softens from its labored breathing into a sigh. Hospice musicians play harp and guitar off to the side of the room, and I remember then one of the sweetest things my father did for me, for us.

He took me to a few R&B concerts before I was old enough to drive. He knew I loved music, hated to talk, and we would sit, basking in the melodies together. The two of us together at small club jams, full of mostly people of color, with Roberta Flack onstage or large auditorium blasts with Donny Hathaway and others. Me and my father, whose six-foot-five frame made him stand out as the only white man around. Even though I felt embarrassed about him at my side, I loved it at the same time, my loving father brave enough to venture out with me this way, even though he lacked courage in some other ways. I loved him and hated him, and in the end, only loved him.

HE DIED THE night of our visit with the baby lamb toy. While we waited for the mortician—my girls and my niece, Madeline, played Crazy Eights with the deck of cards I found in his dresser. Right at the foot of my father's bed, next to his lifeless body, they giggled and shuffled cards. When the mortuary workers arrive, along with my sister-in-law, we all escorted him alongside the gurney, his body in a brown, vinyl body bag like my mother's, down the long nursing-home halls into the parking lot.

Later that night, in the underground parking lot of our apartment building, my oldest daughter, who'd been teaching herself to ride her bike for almost a full year but still couldn't stay upright, hopped on her bike as I reached into the car to take her sister out of the car seat. I turned around and she sailed past me on her bicycle. No training wheels, just free riding on her own. Life not only goes on, it soars, where joy can live inside loss and grief.

MY CHILDREN ARE still young as I begin to write this, and I believe their story is for them to tell, not me, which they've confirmed. Like any parent, I'm protective of them. My world doesn't need to be their world.

As a new mother, I'm not prepared for the pressures of parenting and one day, frustration about something I can't remember erupts. I'm alone at home and strike the edge of my daughter's crib. My right hand fractures into bits. I wonder then if I'll ever stop this fight with myself, with the world. While I'd never dream of placing a hand on one of my girls or anyone else, I want this battle with myself ended. My hand in a pink cast for months, I walk them to pre-school with this constant reminder about my unpredictable inner turmoil. I consult a specialist in trauma and grief, along with another professional who treats soldiers with PTSD, post-traumatic stress disorder. I feel like a soldier, a warrior. I learn that not just soldiers live with PTSD but also survivors of rape and abuse—and inmates.

"Childhood trauma in the first years," they tell me, "overstimulate and enlarge the amygdala, the part of the brain which processes emotion."

It's like I'm in a science class, but I also recognize I need to address my thinking and behavior. I'm afraid of myself right then.

"This part of the brain controls impulses and processes memories of emotions," they say.

Oh hell. I recall the multiple broken attachments and severed bonds I experienced as a child. Then we discuss my discovery of The Letter.

"The shock and trauma pitched you into a tunnel of dissociative amnesia," the counselors say.

The lockdown, my emotions blocked and separated from my body.

"Overdeveloped fight or flight or freeze instinct," one of the professionals says.

They suggest I have PTSD, which started, they say, in my infancy. Lots of people heal from PTSD, though.

There's more. "Most likely you arrived in your adoptive home with RAD," one of the counselors goes on. "Reactive attachment disorder."

The word *disorder* sounds like a prison sentence.

As one of the counselors explains more about this, I'm dazed. "It's a rare and lifelong condition," she says. "And it can permanently change a child's brain in development and hurt her ability to establish future relationships. Often caused by early separation from a birth mother, a child learns subconsciously it's dangerous to attach."

Yikes, it's all there, I think. It's more and more clear what damage those early years caused. But I don't accept it because I'm sure I'll overcome it all.

Signs of RAD in toddlers and children include withdrawal from others, aggressive behavior towards peers, masked feelings of anger, and, the counselor adds, "Watching others closely but not engaging in social interaction, preferring not to be held and to play alone." On and on, and it all rings true.

"A lifelong challenge," the counselor stresses.

Yet I'm almost relieved because now I understand more about my past.

STUDIES SUGGEST THAT chronic intrauterine exposure to heroin causes hyperactivity, a brief attention span, and delayed cognitive, perceptive, and motor skills, as well as other developmental delays such as hypersensitivity to light, sound, and touch. Does this explain my sensory jitters as a girl? Maybe it does explain the occasional pinball of language and sound inside me where at times it's too much for me to drive and talk at the same time, and at other times, when sound and light bounce in a battle for my attention during a group conversation.

More pieces fall together for me during my consultations with childhood specialists. Since every drug a pregnant woman ingests passes from her bloodstream through the placenta to the fetus, drug addiction in a mother causes addiction for the baby. After birth, with the drug no longer available, a baby's central nervous system becomes overstimulated and causes withdrawal symptoms, which can last for two to six months.

I learn how the brain of a deeply traumatized child needs repair over a lifetime, if it's possible. I'd already conquered one: my reaction to the smell of airplanes and the big vomit scenes when I travel. The olfactory bulb communicates right into the amygdala and hippocampus, the latter responsible for associative learning. Both are part of the brain's limbic system, an area connected with memory and feeling, sometimes called the "emotional brain." It's all tight wiring and explains a lot of my past.

The sense of smell often calls up powerful responses and memories in an instant from conditioned past experiences. When we smell a new scent, we link it to an event or a person, even to a moment. Our brains forge a bond between the smell and a memory. When we encounter that smell again, the link is built in, ready to provoke a feeling or association. It's common for smells to call up childhood memories because we encounter most new odors in youth, though studies show we begin to form associations between smell and emotion before we're even born. Infants who were exposed to drugs, alcohol, or cigarette smoke in the womb show a preference for these smells. Even for garlic. Such smells might upset another baby, but to the initiated, they're normal smells, even comforting.

This all explains my nausea on airplanes, the association with the Big Escape.

"Babies who suffer from heroin withdrawal also struggle with eating difficulties, overstimulation, and irritability," a counselor tells me.

I suck in deep breaths. *This was me. She's described my parents' concerns about our first years together.*

"They're difficult to console or comfort."

My heart pumps full with a burst of pain. I don't think about how I needed comfort. *Poor Mother, I couldn't hug her. Wouldn't.*

If only, if only . . . my parents had been informed, our relationship and my childhood could've been so much easier. But now I understand "if only" doesn't go anywhere. I need to reframe my view of the past with a new perspective through a different lens.

I'VE SWITCHED FROM the addict outlaw to a hands-on mom. When my girls reach elementary-school age, I arrange play dates and sleepovers for them. Or we pile together into the car and go to the park, where we zoom down the slide and I push them sky high on the rope swing. Other times I sit in parent-teacher conferences and feel clueless.

As they've gotten older, I oversee their Facebook usage and monitor PG movies. I take my daughters to dance performances, concerts, and museums. Instead of a middle-of-the-night run to the dope dealer, I grab my kids on a Sunday afternoon and after a lunch of buttered noodles, their favorite too, we visit *Veiled Lady* and stroll the museum. We hold hands, and even though I have my two daughters, I long for my mama sometimes. I know she's with us in spirit.

We sit down together for family meals, though not formal or as long as my childhood dinners. Other moms at the school ask how I've taught my children such disciplined study habits, and I just grin. I don't know how, but I know why—I'm haunted by the idea that my kids might run crazy like I did.

One afternoon, I pick up my daughters from school. "We're off to Mexico," I say.

The beach and anywhere on the water is still a place I always long for, and my kids now share this after our travels to Cape Cod, Sanibel, Southern California, the Oregon and Washington coasts, and now Mexico.

They both jump forward in their seats, eyes aglow. "When?" they ask.

"Now!"

They yelp all the way to the airport and the beam never leaves my face. How life can change. My last visit to Mexico, I crossed the border with a car full of weed, bags of coke and white crosses, and a switchblade and gun under my seat. I never thought I'd say it, but now I carry something much more precious than drugs in my car.

CHAPTER TWENTY-TWO

CURIOUS AND WITH PURPOSE

*If you want to awaken all of humanity, then awaken all of
yourself. If you want to eliminate the suffering in the world,
then eliminate all that is dark and negative in yourself.
Truly, the greatest gift you have to give is that of your own
self-transformation. —Lao Tzu*

THE DAY WE ENTER THIS WORLD and the day we discover our purpose—
these two moments bind our lives to meaning. Through the evolu-
tion out of my past, I felt adrift at sea. What do I do with my life
now? More than anything, I've used my curiosity to find purpose
in life. I look for humor and fun as much as I search for serious
meaning. I still roller-skate and dabble in the bass guitar, and I love
boxing. Laughter and play fuel me for the long journey. And there's
always the beach.

Much of my drive for curiosity comes from my parents, most of
all from my mother, who would urge me to notice the world around
me, to look for the beauty in everyday life. Together, curiosity and
the thrill of adventurous living push me through loss and uncertainty and into contentment, and often joy.

Just in recent years do I hear my mother's voice follow me around
with its reminder "Look around," as she'd say on Sunday drives to
the Japanese garden in Seattle. She'd call attention to the quiver of
dry grasses in a breeze or a hummingbird in its hover around sugar
water in our kitchen-window feeder. She encouraged me to pay attention to details around us the times she joined my father's and my
excursions to the public market on Seattle's waterfront. "Look at the

red on this pomegranate," I remember her saying. Or, "Do you like this texture?" and she'd pick up an artichoke. She'd wrap her arm around my shoulder and we'd lean together to watch birds squabble and peck for crumbs at the market entry.

I recall one day on a walk by the market through the park where a lot of homeless people stayed, and she pointed out the beauty of the lines in an old woman's hands, folded across her lap. While my mother showed compassion, I also learned another lesson from her about inequities in life.

Just in recent days I've recalled her letters from the ten or so years I was estranged from my parents, after I'd moved out at seventeen, when, as Mother called me, I was a hoodlum. She'd write to me in her minuscule fountain-pen script, "Send me a note, write anything. Tell me what the sky looks like at night or about the fall leaf colors."

I can't pinpoint the exact moment I started to "look around," yet over time, my view of the world changed. Curiosity replaced my life of drugs, crime, and thrill seeking. It's this curiosity about the world and other people, this need to explore outside of myself, that saved me. Rather than holding onto an apathetic and stagnant world view about my surroundings, I focus on the next best step, excited about the unknown even if I'm afraid of it. Whatever it is, I take a step. Whether it's forward or even a step to the side or backward, I step.

My mothers, each in a different way, taught me to embrace life and to stand strong when the world shakes. I'm grateful to my prison mom for the spirit of this tug of opposites and how it stirs in me. From her, beyond the addiction we shared, beyond the year in prison, I inherited a restless, wild fire that burns in my soul, one I'm sure she also carried.

My whole life I've wrestled with my prison roots, my adoption, and my identity. But don't we all tweak our identity a bit as we go along? A new relationship, marriage, divorce, the death of someone we love, birth, adoption, financial or job change, a move to a new city—every part of the life cycle is a chance for personal transformation. I learned this the hard way as I dismantled myself, brick by brick, until I could look through new eyes, something that took decades after I'd read the letter and drank the Kool-Aid of secrecy and toxic shame. I'd committed emotional suicide. After everything, I needed to take control of my own identity because chronic suffering is a place with no future and staying there was slow death.

THE ONCE-MUTE GIRL who shunned attention, I begin a career as a public speaker. The stage terrifies me. Why would I put myself in the position I've hated all my life: people looking at me. My eleven-year-old daughter finds her own wisdom in my journey. One day I pick her up after school and we discuss my return to prisons as a speaker. She says, "I think it means your spirit is free."

Public speaking pushes me past my safety zone and I enjoy this challenge. Whether by nature or because I crave adventure, I love the exploration through unmapped territory. It's fun, it's scary.

I speak in public about my journey because I'm a storyteller and a writer with a purpose, not because I was born in prison. At first, to overcome my fear of talking, I'd take a deep breath and repeat a mantra I'd practiced all my life but never with intention until recent years: *Go. Do it.* I told myself the same thing when I stood outside my prison mother's cell, except then I couldn't follow through on it. I said the same thing when Mother was dying.

My former enemies are now clients who invite me to keynote conferences for professionals in law enforcement and corrections, mental health care, social work, adoption, foster care, and other social services. The first time I keynoted at an adoption conference, I came face to face with the pain birth mothers feel. I had never witnessed their anguish and our shared "what ifs." I left there with deep compassion for their yearning and loss. Then, last year, the agency that placed me out of foster care invited me to keynote for their annual fund-raiser, and I'm told it raised more money than any other year.

Once again I'm a poster girl, yet this time I'm an example of what the other side of "at-risk and special needs" looks like. Most of all, I present myself as proof that anyone can overcome obstacles. With caution, I tug the crime-and-drug saga out of the pinhole pocket in my brain, along with the family stories. I talk about how I made it out alive, resilient, reinvented. At one particular speaking engagement, after I tell pieces of my story to a group of psychologists, one raises her hand.

"How did you change?" she asks. I'd mentioned the plot to gas my parents, along with a few life-threatening exploits. "Today, if one of us called the Mayo Clinic to seek consultation about a child with the kind of behavior you describe, they'd refuse to treat you and your family. I doubt they'd admit a child with the symptoms you describe."

"What? Why?" I ask.

Her answer shocks me. "It's untreatable," she says, "the extreme danger you presented to others, the attachment disorder, PTSD as an infant, RAD, the violence. That's why I asked how you changed."

AS FOR ATTACHMENT disorder and other diagnostic labels related to trauma, today I don't link myself to any of them. I don't claim them, even though I might struggle with the symptoms. I shun labels. Even prison baby. Whatever I am, I am—and I continue to grow and evolve because sometimes where we've been broken is where we free ourselves the most.

The group discussion caused me to understand that I was never alone, even in the times I thought so. We don't have maps for loss. Mentors, coaches, teachers, neighbors, family, friends, partners, all who walk the path with us, they help shape our lives when there's no algorithm to follow. I'm the only one, though, to decide if I listen to others and work and push forward—to learn, to forgive, to flourish.

I focus most on my prison tours, and to embody this work, two significant colleagues and mentors, now board members, helped me form a nonprofit organization, the unPrison Project. At least once a month I travel to a prison in a different state to address gyms full of inmates who sit on rows of folding chairs, the walls lined with guards. I turn over my personal belongings at the gate. Steel doors clang behind me, and hundreds, often thousands, of women await me on the inside. My work as a speaker is not a verb. It's a social justice and spiritual act. Judaism calls this *tikkun olam*, "to repair the world." If we lock up rather than heal, treat, and alter behavior, then the United States will remain the industrialized country that incarcerates the most people. I believe healing, not prison cells, will change our massive incarceration—if we invest in health and wellness, in restorative measures and rehabilitation.

Mental health care is a commonsense solution to help reduce incarceration, child abuse, and domestic violence. We can pay for these problems up front or pay even more on the back end, in our schools, jails, and prisons.

Part of the dialogue I engage in with inmates is about forgiveness—for ourselves and others. But how do we forgive the unforgivable, and why would we? Another lifelong journey.

Freedom and healing are humanitarian issues. Is our system one of justice or vengeance, or of healing and rehabilitation? Incarceration is a serious concern for our society. The majority of prison sentences relate to crimes stemming from drug-related charges, as in the case of my biological mother. Many prison officials say that the majority of incarcerated women also have diagnosable mental health issues. Common sense says, then, that the best route to a healed and safe society is treatment, rehab, and education as alternatives to incarceration.

Eleven states now house nurseries on their prison compounds. Some studies find that babies who remain with their mothers grow up with healthy attachments, and for the mothers, their rate of recidivism decreases. On the other hand, some people dispute whether a child is better off removed at birth so that attachment to an incarcerated woman doesn't develop. My belief is every case is unique.

The rapid increase of incarceration of women is an international concern, as much as it is for the children born inside and those left behind while a mother serves her sentence. Trinidad, Canada, Australia, China—all are countries where women's prison populations are on the rise and therefore deep concerns arise for the children left behind. A number of prisons in other countries have reached out to me in recent months, and I'm driven to expand this work of mentorship and life-skills programs for incarcerated women and girls. Established nursery programs in prisons in other countries allow children and babies to stay with their mothers. After years of working in the field, I've learned that Cambodia's prison system allows children of inmates to stay with their incarcerated mothers until age three. Ghana permits female inmates to keep their children, with certain restrictions, and in Johannesburg, South Africa, sometimes up to thirty toddlers live with their incarcerated mothers. Now, my vision clear with a greater sense of purpose, I hope to reach the people in these international prisons as well as more across the United States.

Either way, we need solutions because more and more inmates are pregnant at time of sentencing. The need is high for how to address the incarcerated parent-child dilemma.

CHAPTER TWENTY-THREE

FREEDOM ON THE INSIDE

EACH TIME I LEAVE A PRISON it's as if I've left a war zone of the soul, hundreds and hundreds of wounded souls. Afterward I need a power wash of my own so I can reconnect into my world a little less charred. I go in alone and come out crowded, flooded with stories and sorrows. More and more, after every prison visit, I'm disconnected from day-to-day life. It's a new kind of emotional lockdown, although it's really more of a pause, to take in the bigness of what I witness, to allow it all to sift through me.

I'll goof around on Facebook, Twitter, and other social media playgrounds because I can't focus on anything else. My writing, my art, my family and friends—my world—float far away from me. I struggle to integrate my worlds, my private day-to-day with the intensity of my public life, and most of all, the fierce nature of my prison work. I battle to find balance, to shift back and forth between my life of writing, family, and friends, and the powerful soul connections I build in prisons.

I've learned from several therapists in their "shop talk" that an estimated 10 percent of a client's "stuff" sticks to the therapist— the stories, the energy, the problems. I'm not a therapist, but the energy from the thousands of inmates I meet, and from staff and management, soaks into me, along with the stories of their families and communities.

Overall, what I've collected from dozens of prisons and thousands of incarcerated women could fill a warehouse, a city, a world of other women's trauma, sorrow, and loss. After facing gyms full of incarcerated women and girls ranging from ages eleven to eighty-five—yes, I've met girls this young in youth prisons—I understand how we share a humanity, inside prison or out. These top ten questions arise wherever I speak:

1. "What do I do with the pain?"
2. "Where will I find support after I leave?"
3. "How does spirituality fit into making life changes?"
4. "How can I find relief from the guilt?"
5. "How long does it take to figure out a purpose?"
6. "Will my children ever end their anger with me?"
7. "What makes you think you can do what you do?"
8. "I'm losing my children, my family. What do I do now?"
9. "How do I handle the fear of change?"
10. "I'm not sure: do all secrets need telling?"

Who of us out hasn't wondered some of these same things? In fact, when I keynote at a conference of professionals, attendees often ask some of the same questions. I can't offer absolute answers because I don't think there are any when it comes to emotion. I just know my story, how I've learned to walk in this world of beauty with all its uncertainty.

My work now is to turn myself into more of a sieve and make sure I renew myself in between each prison tour.

GRIEF AND UNCERTAINTY trapped me for most of my life. What if my attempts to eliminate those two feelings had been my real prison?

Maybe I've asked myself the wrong questions all along. What if the fight against sorrow, fear, and uncertainty confines us in misery? A wall of fear and resentment, not a bricks-and-mortar prison, had constricted me, even though I was free.

After all those years of anguish, maybe I needed to start asking, "What can I do to feel deep contentment with life on life's terms?"

Beneath everything I'd struggled through lay a path of seeking happiness. It's a multibillion-dollar industry: self-help and the happiness quest. And I dove in. I've tried positive thinking, visualizing goals and dreams, hypnotherapy, every self-help book and trend, to transform myself, to change my thoughts and feelings—and I learned much from all of it.

But what if we change the premise? Maybe we're all hooked on a flawed goal, like addicts in pursuit of the next fix, looking for a quick release.

As a culture we're led to believe we must reconcile everything. We're a now culture, a fix-it culture. I for one am a right-now person. We aim for reconciliation, and we want it right away. We kick into resolve-now mode in a desire to make everything better. We demand solutions for climate change, for social justice, for political rightness, for a better economy, increased gun safety. We demand solutions, and we want them right now.

Happiness appears, then hides, a moving target, while contentment, when we find it, is for keeps. My search for ways to ward off the discomfort of uncertainty and sorrow—the drugs, excessive drinking, the jump from relationship to relationship, the marathon run away from my demons—kept me locked up. Not my prison birth, not foster care, not my adoption, not the racism and sexism around me, not my struggle about faith and spirituality, not the bad relationships, not the worries of motherhood, not betrayal by family members, not the stretches of poverty in my life, not the loss of businesses and housing.

Even after I cleaned up and changed my lifestyle, my new world brought a different kind of entrapment—overwork and a search for perfection, for happiness targets, and goals like excessive workouts at the gym, the drive for more money, more property, more acceptance by my peers. More more more. I always yearned for what was ahead, which was never enough if I always steered away from the present moment.

No matter where we are, now is all we have.

The exact conditions I battled to avoid—the grip of loss, sorrow, and uncertainty—freed me to live fully, to taste life's rich flavors.

I continue to live with uncertainty. I'm still in search of information about my birth father and about which boxes to check for race other than "multiracial." I've now discovered through DNA tests that I'm part Taiwanese, in addition to being part Greek and part Latina, plus—as my prison documents revealed—the possible "one drop of blood." Now, rather than an outcast, I'm a perfect palette of paints, part of the new multiracial demographic. According to the 2010 US Census, the trend indicates that one in every five Americans will be multiracial by the year 2050. In a few decades I'll be in the majority.

I continue to live in uncertainty about my race and about how I was conceived. Given my prison mother's lifestyle, for all I know, I could be the product of rape, of prostitution, of a one-night stand, or of a weeklong affair. I put some of these questions out of my mind. Instead, I hold dear the year my birth mother and I shared in our palace.

We live in a culture that pushes us to think of happiness as an end goal. When I lived in Tokyo, I remember one of my Japanese friends asked me why in the West people focused on happiness as an objective. I didn't have any answer for her. By this time I'd already shifted my focus away from happiness and looked to contentment for the best place to rest.

But I used to. Along the way, I set happiness markers and clung to them as if each one would rescue me:

When I graduate high school.

When I turn eighteen.

When I move to another city.

When I quit drugs.

When I quit drinking.

When I find the right partner.

When I buy a house and find a better job.

When I make more money.

When I dye my hair, or I lighten my skin, or when it darkens more from the sun . . .

I had no idea how loss and pain, if grieved, could lead to contentment, even if it took twenty years to mourn. I can't identify the exact moment it happened, when a vastness opened inside me like a torrent of warm summer rain and cleansed any doubts I held whether I could go on living with the sorrow.

Yes, I'm happy today, and for no specific reason at all I'm filled with joy. If I'm sad and sorrowful at times for whatever comes about, in the same moments I can feel contentment and find humor and joy. *Sorrowjoy*, because if we sit still inside and let it in, they live together and we thrive.

CHAPTER TWENTY-FOUR

THEN, THIS

THE TRUTH IS . . . MY LIFE IS GOOD. I'm lucky for life itself, to have out-lived the lineup of harrowing escapades. Best of all, I've made peace with the family I rejected for so long. I'm grateful for each second, third, and fourth chance at life, grateful for all those who've stood by, who believed in me.

One day several years ago I applied for life insurance, something to add a little security for my family. I'm a mother after all. I'm supposed to think of these things. My father didn't believe in life insurance—he said he didn't want anyone to profit from his death. Why not, though?

I MAKE AN appointment to fill out a life insurance application, and when the nurse shows up at my studio office with the form, she draws a little blood and asks me a series of questions, none of them memorable.

A week later she calls. "Deborah, we have to decline you for life insurance. Your liver enzymes measured six times the normal level."

Liver enzymes? What the hell is that? The last time I heard the word *enzyme* was in high school chemistry. I'm in perfect health, toned from working out, and feel great, other than the exhaustion I have all the time. Since I've cleaned up, I've never even had a headache and can count on one hand the times a flu or cold struck me. Even with little kids, after I got the mandatory colds they bring home from pre-school, I've been immune to every seasonal bug.

The nurse goes on. "You should call a doctor."

I'm at my desk and the autumn sun slashes through the window at my back and casts its yellow onto the teak desk, the one my father used in his study. Now it's mine, cluttered like when it was his, with piles of paper stacked into geodesic configurations.

"Immediately," she adds.

My heart jackhammers into my throat. I ask her what it all means, and she says, "I'm not allowed to diagnose or discuss any more details." Which frightens me even more.

I don't remember if I asked any more questions. It starts again, my habit of emotional lockdown.

It turns out I have chronic hepatitis C, an incurable liver virus, similar to HIV/AIDS in that it's transmitted by blood and, I'll say again, incurable. The liver biopsy—a stab with a foot-long needle to core the liver and analyze the sample—showed I'm in midstage. I've never asked stage of what, because I feel fine.

I'm a mother of two small children and carry this invincible feeling like I'm still a teen—time will never end and there's no limit to life. I'd been born into loss, and after two decades to break its shackles, I've worked hard to build a filter for impulse control and to catch up from emotional delays of early trauma and a lifetime of drug abuse. Now this?

I survived death-defying feats, unprotected sex, and a risky lifestyle. I'd stood up after sorrow sent me to the mat, flat on my back. At last I am serious about life and about living and staying alive, and now, I'm face-to-face with the possibility of death.

I can't stop my mind from spinning. *How did I contract this? Did it happen because I shared needles as a former IV-drug user? Or did the tattoo artist in San Diego at the street-side dive use a dirty needle on me? Or is it one more legacy from my birth mother? Did she pass it on to me in her womb?*

I've never heard of hep C. Now what? I hit the Internet, a double-edged razor because there are facts, and then opinions posted as facts. The web offers as much of both.

More than four million in the United States and 170 million around the globe have hepatitis C, according to the World Health Organization. It's a sleeper disease, often with no symptoms. If I'd never applied for life insurance, I'd probably never have found out about it. If I'd kept drinking and ingesting drugs, I'd have keeled over a long time ago. Some of what I learned about symptoms helps explain the deep fatigue I've felt. However, I'm a mother who needs much more than young children to tug her into exhaustion.

MY BODY TALKED to me for years, maybe even the stomach bleeding from my drug days and then, later, the loss of appetite, fatigue, muscle aches, occasional nausea, abdominal pain, jaundice, generalized itching, most of these I'd experienced. The progression of the disease into later stages can mean liver scarring, which leads to cirrhosis. Late-stage signs include vomiting, an altered mental state, stupor or coma, internal bleeding. Most of these I'd experienced before, induced by street drugs. Not to make light of this but still . . .

Later stages can lead to dire circumstances, ones I can't even put on paper or discuss because I am determined to focus on quality of life and not my diagnosis. Or maybe I just can't face reality. I was never good at this. Not until I'm forced to by, well, the dire circumstances.

Here it is again, stigma. Only now it's the stigma of an infectious disease. I already know about living with an incurable disease, addiction, but this is different.

How will I ever get past the feeling that I'm tainted? This time it's literal. My blood is tainted with a virus. I can't ever donate blood, and when I get a cut, I need to make sure no one touches the area, especially if the person has an open wound.

I'm forced to figure out how to live with an incurable disease, how to remain positive through it all. Incurable for now. Our world changes at a fast pace, and who knows, any day someone might discover a cure.

As much as family and friends want to help, it's still hard for anyone to understand what it feels like to live with an incurable disease unless you're living with one. I think of Mother and am glad she's not around to learn about this. She'd fret, which would then make me fret. No mother wants her child faced with a health issue. I think of Mother during her illness and dying, how I knew she felt afraid. I could see it in her eyes and yet we never talked about fear. I am my mothers' daughter, both of them. I choose to shift through and beyond the fear.

I learn the hard way about support groups when I attend one for people living with hep C, sponsored by Hazelden, celebrated for their chemical-dependency treatment program. I figured it's a known brand, so why not? At first when I walk into the room, I plop into a cushioned chair off to the side. Everyone else has pulled up a metal folding chair in a rough circle. I'm still shy in groups and sit alone.

A facilitator begins with his introduction, then we go around the circle of about twenty or so people, and each one gives a brief overview of her- or himself. Most people talked about their interferon treatments and about their fear of dying and of feeling nauseated.

I refuse interferon because I understand it replicates chemo with its side effects of depression, a possible relapse into addiction, and suicidal tendencies, all of which can last for more than a year. Great, a treatment with side effects worse than my symptoms, which are few. No thank you.

My doctor persists in trying to persuade me to undergo this treatment, and after months of feeling pressured by him, I find a different doctor who practices East-West medicine. I feel healthy and take herbal and Eastern medicines, along with doing shiatsu and other muscle-healing approaches to relax.

When it's my turn to speak in the group's first meeting, I say, "I never think about hepatitis day to day." I paused, shift in my seat, scared of the silence. "In fact, half the time I forget it."

All eyes stare at me. No one says a word, and the person next to me doesn't begin his turn.

None of them, of course, knows about my ability to tuck something away in a little pocket in the back of my mind when I don't want to think about it. This time it serves me well. I figure that if I focus on the disease, I won't heal just by worrying about it. So why worry?

The facilitator turns to the others. "How does everyone feel about Deborah's denial?"

Huh? Denial? I didn't say this.

I don't remember anything that happens after this because I sink into my lockdown mode, feeling exposed, alone, and vulnerable. As soon as the group ends its two-hour session, I bolt and never return. Good thing I've learned to go with my instinct and trust what doesn't feel right. This group was the wrong place for me.

There's no one right way to live, and no right way to live with a diagnosis. It's a good idea to focus on a healthy lifestyle, and maybe it's a time to think about personal growth and life's bigger meaning. Still, how we react is a personal choice.

Soon after the diagnosis, my mind races with all sorts of thoughts. *What about my future? Have I lived as well as I could? What about sex? Do I stop my dreams—are they over? I just started to dream big! I'm scared. My kids! What about my darlings, their little-girl lives ahead of them and their mama . . .*

I can't fill in the blank. Their mama, what?

I have my children tested, and neither of them carries any sign of the virus.

In a way, at first I take the diagnosis as if it were payback time, as if I'd been handed a life sentence. At the same time, my attitude is, fuck everything and treasure everything.

Then, flash! I recall something from high school. Right after one of my annual physicals, my mother had said, "The doctor called. You need to return for another test."

I was old enough to drive by then, so I zipped back to the doctor's office. All I remember is when the results came back to my mother, she reported: "They said your urine looked like you might have hepatitis or something like that."

I remember precisely the word *hepatitis*. I never looked it up and thought it was some boring word related to health. I'm seventeen after all, and what girl, especially the kind I was, pays attention to her mother or doctor?

"Drink lots of water," my mother said, almost as a scold and a command.

But there was no more discussion and I never asked one question.

With the new diagnosis, the thought flickers through my mind: *Did I inherit this from my mother in prison?* In utero transmission is infrequent. Infrequent but not impossible. So is a baby born in prison, infrequent.

My next thought surprises me: "My mothers are killing me. One from secrecy, the other with tainted blood."

But this drama moment passed right away because my new muscles for rational thinking kicked in. I'll never find out how I contracted this, and I can't get lost in the "what if . . ." I never take the route of victim, so all I'm left with is the stance of warrior, away from the path of suffering. It's the default I choose as a woman, to veer away from the old story of victim and create a new one where we are warriors, brave and soft in our courage even when afraid.

The diagnosis launches me onto a familiar road—the unknown, an adventure. *Fight this damn thing.* I pull on my *Well, then, let's see what happens* boots, and I'm ready to take this on. Inside, I both brace myself and soften into this new awareness. Instead of thinking, "I have an incurable, chronic disease," I use the language, "I've been diagnosed with hepatitis C, and so far there's no cure."

Tomorrow isn't here yet, so who knows what discovery might develop. Or not discovered. Either way, if I worry today about tomorrow, then I'll miss the moments of Right Now, of living with no urge to step away or towards anything. True contentment. It may sound glib, yet I live this to my core, and it's easier since I don't take life for granted.

THE AFTERSHOCK OF my diagnosis has lifted and I've been living symptom-free with no medications. When I participated in a National Institutes of Health blind study of Chinese herbs for treatment, my viral count reduced. I turn to all kinds of relaxing bodywork when I can, like acupuncture, shiatsu, yoga stretches, whatever I need to take charge of my health. I don't think about this diagnosis every day. In fact, for months and months the thought never crosses my mind.

Every *I love you, I'm sorry, forgive me, I forgive you* sits in my mouth with a new taste. Every *thank-you* rolls off my lips with deeper meaning. I'm not diseased, not impaired. I'm just aware of which organ might fail on me, or might not. Or a taxicab might run me over next week, too. It's this random, life. I'm not suggesting it's best to ignore something so serious. It's just that I've put the diagnosis in its place, off into a little pocket in the back of my brain. I'm aware it's there. The pocket isn't closed. It's got a fancy abalone-shell button ready for me to pry open with gentleness whenever I need to.

I've told some of my family and friends, but for many who read it here, this will be the first time they find out. Once in a while those in my inner circle ask me, "How's your health?" and I tell them all is well.

Every year around my birthday I get a blood test to monitor any changes and a CT scan of my liver area to check for enlargement. So far, nothing. If I postpone the annual test, any one of my friends will encourage me to get on it. Each report after the annual test, rather than go over the details of my enzyme and viral count, the doctor calls and says, "Your enzymes are high, expected for someone with hepatitis C. Nothing to cause alarm, though."

And I'm not alarmed. Every morning I wake up eager for my day, especially since I'm less and less secretive about this diagnosis. If Mother were still alive, I might not have wanted to tell her at first, but eventually I would. Sometimes the need to keep a secret is to protect ourselves, and sometimes it's to protect others. I've now shared the basics of this diagnosis with my children, enough so they're informed and enough not to scare them. A mother's natural urge is to shelter the ones she loves from a truth that might hurt or cause fear.

CHAPTER TWENTY-FIVE

FROZEN IN TIME

"ANY QUESTIONS?" I ASK IN A prison gym filled with women.

"Yeah," one of the inmates asks. "Are you angry with your mother in prison?"

The question stops me cold.

I stand in the gym below the stage, eye level with the rows of prisoners. Several hundred forest-green-clad women stare at me, waiting for my answer.

I've been stunned into silence before. Once an inmate called out to me from the back row in an echoing gym full of three hundred women. She rose to her feet, her weeping so fierce I couldn't understand one word. She repeated the sentence over and over and then I heard it: "Tomorrow social services pulls my daughter out of foster care, and then she's adopted. I'm losing her! I'm losing her!" She asked, "What do I do?"

Before I knew it, others began to weep. Buried grief surged to the surface in a tidal wave, and I stood alone on the front line.

This woman didn't need an answer from me; she just sought comfort, and a mother losing her daughter is inconsolable.

RIGHT NOW, WITH this inmate who asks about anger, I stand alone again on the front line. *Angry with my prison mother?* I'd searched deep into the quietest cave of my soul to wonder why I'd never felt angry toward her. Wouldn't a child burn inside with fury about a mother

164

who abandoned her? Wouldn't a girl separated from her mother wonder what was wrong?

Children cry and rage when their mothers leave just to go to the grocery store. Babies demand, *Don't leave me! Come back!* while their mothers pull away for a quick errand, leaving a babysitter or spouse in charge. Yet a baby wants her mama. Sometimes my daughters wailed when they were infants whenever I took off for a much-needed night out, so I know.

But have I never felt angry with Margo? I've asked myself this hundreds of times. Who delivers a baby in prison and keeps her for a year? Maybe she thought she could raise me in prison until her release. But for years? For her whole sentence? My adult brain knows I might be mad at her for not cleaning up. Why couldn't she stay out of prison? What did she think would happen, running the streets with junk in her veins while pregnant with me?

The Bureau of Prisons documents revealed just facts, information I processed in my head. My bond with my birth mother, though, this lives in my heart, a love frozen in time. Prison protected us, walled us into our cocoon. Prison gave us a home together. Our palace.

It's hard to hold much anger about her if the first year is all I hug inside my heart. I never expected her to change anything in our year. She kept me. She loved me, and I loved her. I feel protective of her. I once listened to a forensic psychologist interviewed on the news one night who said that sometimes when someone is demonized, those who love the person will make that person into a saint. From the moment I read about my prison mother, I already knew the public perception of women in prison, in fact, of anyone incarcerated. They're second-class citizens. I'm here to defy those judgments. Every human being is worthy of love no matter what's happened, where we come from, or where we've been.

It may sound nuts to someone on the outside, but if this first year is all I have with her, then it's flawless. We were perfect.

The neurologist Oliver Sacks explores memory in his book *Hallucinations* and presents what I've witnessed and know is true from my preverbal memory and infant life in prison: "We now know that memories are not fixed or frozen, like Proust's jars of preserves in a larder, but are transformed, disassembled, reassembled, and re-categorized with every act of recollection."

When we don't have a lot of memories, we protect the few we hold. For my prison mom—what I hold inside is frozen in time. Forever. I'll never create another memory. For Mother and me—we had the gift of chance after chance to build new memories.

All I share with my prison mother are my restless spirit, our physical features, my yarn toy, and sensory memories. What else do I have with her? Nothing. Not one thing. Why tarnish these few treasures, taint the softness of our year together? We shared so little time that I don't want any anger to shroud this perfect love we shared.

But, but . . . wait a minute. This question from the inmate triggers a tornado in my gut.

My prison mom—*Fuck her sorry-ass junkie self,* the girl ripped away from her rages inside.

Fuck. Her.

FUCK YOU—right to Margo's face—*fuck you all locked up in your stupid little steel cell. Why'd you ruin everything?* What kinda mom are you? *Go ahead, rot the rest of your stupid life in prison. See if I care.*

But I care. A boulder of ache blasts a hole through my chest, a bloody mess of sorrow splattered everywhere.

If anything, I'm angry at the series of events that I now know are the reason why I lashed out against the world at large, a world unfair in its dealings, where my whole emotional world of brokenness stirred at work underground, out of control. I've surrendered any hope for a different past or story.

I don't have words for the fury and sadness I can still feel at irregular times about the circumstances and separation. They puncture my heart. The rage can drop me to my knees, shattered, and then batters me some more, because if I stopped, I'd blow up in bits. A whole book and a bunch of published essays don't touch the sorrow of these moments, but if I stayed only where I felt comfortable, that zone would have turned into a self-built barricade. Every step of the way, I've inched out of my comfort zone, just a little at a time.

CHAPTER TWENTY-SIX

BEAUTIFUL UNCERTAIN WORLD

THE AUTHORITIES AND GOVERNMENT OFFICIALS INVOLVED in the web of my custody and my future, from West Virginia to Washington, DC, to Seattle, what were they supposed to do with a baby in prison? Let me serve my mother's ten-year sentence with her?

My Margo mother, what could she do? Raise me with my one yarn toy and her village—two hundred inmates along with guards and a warden for my community? A baby needs exposure to the big beautiful uncertain world. A baby needs a community to surround her with stimulation, colors, and texture. A baby needs more than just miles and miles of cotton khaki. I love color, a luscious and vibrant world, most of all, any shade of sunshine yellow. Yet I imagine just inmate and guard uniforms surrounded me for my first year.

I'm conflicted. A baby also yearns for her first bond, and a year-long one, even more.

Just one emotion floods me, all mushed together, whenever I think of my prison mother and leaving her—anguish and sorrow accompanied by joy. Agony for the separation she and I endured, and joy for no specific memory, just a sensation of our beautiful, short life together—sorrowjoy. I am shredded to pieces by the leaving. My leaving. I left my mom behind, locked up. This one moment in my life—my birth in prison, my prison mom's incarceration and her pregnant behind walls, and then our separation—it all makes me nauseated with grief and love, all a jumble in the pit of my gut. This is what I cannot reconcile.

Ask me if I wish I could've stayed with her, I'll tell you: Yes, forever, for the rest of my life.

Ask me if I'm glad they removed me from prison, I'll tell you: Yes, otherwise I would not be the woman I am today.

You can't breathe and not breathe at the same time.

If healing hitches to us only when we restore harmony inside, then we're misled by the concept of healing and reconciliation. It's not easy, but it is possible to heal even in the midst of discord. One reason it took me so long to get this story on paper is I waited to restore inner harmony, but grief isn't a straight line.

I waited for the day when grief would heal, waited for reconciliation of these messy beautiful feelings about my birth in prison. I waited for sorrow to finish its flood, for sadness to subside, and for my deep-seated unease about the enigma of my prison birth to morph into acceptance. But reconciliation never showed up at my door.

I hoped for a sureness about my start in life, and it never came.

Maybe some experiences we don't need to go away. Maybe we just need to metabolize and integrate them, to get a few stakes in the ground to navigate by. Sometimes the monsters inside us win, and sometimes they don't. For sure we don't need to let them take control and possess us. Identity is whatever we make for ourselves, and not everything ends in resolution. To this day I'm still a restless woman, on fire inside, a low slow burn of healing and contentment now replaces the past flames of rage.

One thing I've reconciled at last and for certain: I do not reconcile my prison birth and all its impact. And I am in love with this commotion inside. It feeds my creativity, my love and joy for life, how I've learned to live in the moment, and my ability to endure uncertainty. All of which give my world beauty and power.

This stir of uncertainty also feeds my love for two mothers. One, a woman I cannot remember with my eyes but sense in my soul. The other, a mother I battled and loved with equal fierceness.

One of life's beautiful challenges is to embrace our own nature, our destiny, even if part of the quest is to accept what we wish we could change—but can't. Nothing brings greater freedom than the discovery of how to live with the unlivable.

THE DAY AFTER MOTHER'S DEATH, I open her cedar trunk and dig through her linens to rescue my yarn toy. Under folded white napkins and her stash of two unopened boxes of Dunhill and Gauloise cigarettes, packed deeper in the trunk, I discover three baby sweaters, one in sunshine yellow with fuzzy mothball-sized pom-pom tassels. More from my prison mom's knitted craftwork, reclaimed at last, pieces of our bond. Today they overlook me, folded, on an open shelf behind my desk.

In the main hallway in my home, the yarn puppy perches on top of an ornate scrolled wall sconce. Beside it leans Mother's Mont Blanc fountain pen, the one she wrote poetry with. Icons of my once-fractured self now unite side by side. This is me, a tapestry of these stories, every bit of confusion worth the contentment and joy I've learned to mine from uncertainty, every battle worth the exploration.

ACKNOWLEDGMENTS

MANY PEOPLE HELPED THIS BOOK COME TO LIFE: Gayatri Patnaik, deep gratitude for your fierce belief in this project and bringing out the best in my work; Rachael Marks, Travis Dagenais, Tom Hallock, Susan Lumenello, Beth Collins, Marcy Barnes, Jessie Bennett, and the rest of the Beacon Press team who worked on my behalf with personal attention and energy to make this book a reality, thank you.

How can I name each person who's touched this work? For the countless people who assisted in this book over so many years, please see yourself in here. Great appreciation goes to every mentor, writing coach, and freelance editor, for teaching me and cheering me on in this project. I'd like to thank all those who helped with research and early readers of my manuscript. I'm grateful for friends and family who provided moral support and helped fuel the creation of this book. Online friends and Facebookers for such loyal virtual support, thank you. My biological family, for all the ways you've embraced me and the story as I tell it, my deepest thanks. Those who take great care of my children when I travel to prisons or need solitude to write, you are our village.

The women and girls I've met in prison, and the ones still to come, it's a privilege to stand before you and see your trust and courage and face your openness in my presence. You are the reason I do this work.

My children offer great patience with my work, and they inspire me every day with reminders about the complexity of motherhood and family. Girls, thanks for the magic.

Enduring love and honor for my parents, who helped shape me into the woman I am today.

Last but not least, high esteem for my mother-source in prison who handed me this story and, because I didn't get a chance before to say it, "Thank you for the yarn toy."